SURVEY OF AFRO-AMERICAN EXPERIENCE
IN THE U.S. ECONOMY

Survey of Afro-American Experience in the U.S. Economy

Martin O. Ijere

An Exposition-University Book
EXPOSITION PRESS
HICKSVILLE, NEW YORK

To
my loving wife,
Muriel

CONTENTS

*The ideas of economists and political philosophers,
both when they are right and when they are wrong,
are more powerful than is commonly understood.
Indeed, the world is ruled by little else.*

J. M. KEYNES

PREFACE

The interest in Black Studies in America today is a clear indication that a veritable field of study should be given its rightful place in the curriculum of educational institutions and in the nation's history. These studies focus attention on all aspects of the people's live, their problems and achievements. Through political science, economics, history, psychology, and other disciplines, the different experiences of the Afro-American are investigated and evaluated in the light of the American economy in particular and that of the world in general. So far economics has received the least treatment from researchers, teachers, and the public, even though this should be among the most fundamental concerns.

The aim of this book is to highlight the principal areas of black contribution in American economic development. It aims further at throwing up new ideas in this hitherto neglected field for further consideration and investigation. Above all, the book is intended to present as clearly as possible the factors that have affected the Afro American's economic life since 1619.

The book begins with a theoretical discussion of the nature and scope of economic history and the basis for the emphasis on the economic factor. Three primary techniques of studying economic history—*traditional, comparative,* and *quantitative*—are distinguished, while the qualities necessary for an economic history investigation are examined. The chapter closes with a discussion of the tools of analysis, the place and interdependence of economic history, economics, and economic growth as well as the various sources for the study of black economic history.

Chapter two throws light on the African background and

illustrates by examples the great economic organizations and achievements of the early empires of Ghana, Mali, and Songhay in such sectors as agriculture, industry, mining, and commerce. The situation in the New World can then be measured against the experience in Africa of an earlier period.

In chapter three, there is an attempt to deal with the important question of black contribution in agriculture. Considered are labor organization, housing, medical care, crop production, and the profitability of the plantation system. Statistics are used where appropriate to substantiate the evidences adduced for the results achieved. In the same way the influences of tenancy and sharecropping on efficiency are examined in chapter four. The first is compared with the African system of slavery in order to illustrate how different results were produced there. In the second, the experiences of the blacks after emancipation are studied as they give clues to the later problems that were to form the permanent aspects of black poverty in this country.

Then follows a detailed investigation into the various transformations that American agriculture has undergone in the last century and the place of blacks within these changes.

Chapter five sets out to explore the black experience in industry. Considered are the problems of capital, scale of operations, and lines of production. For illustrative purposes black economic organizations such as banking and insurance institutions are dealt with and their impact analyzed.

Chapter six explores the shifts in the American economy and how the minority sector is disadvantageously affected in terms of population growth, labor force participation, employment, and standards of living. It further examines the role of black women in the labor force, the forces that give them the comparatively significant role they play in the family and the economy, the occupational experience of black professionals, and the effects of unionization on black employment.

Entrepreneurship is not limited to the realm of capital, organization, and management. It extends to ideas, inventions, and innovations. It is in this context that certain black inventors and innovators, for example, are studied and their impact on the economic life of the country estimated. Not to be ignored are the philosophies of black leaders who through the centuries have pointed the way for the improvement of the lot of Afro-Americans in the American society. It is in this context that chapter seven attempts to describe and evaluate such economic ideas and programs in regards to the historical realities of the time.

A nation's level of living is derived from the educational level of its citizens. This is because education plays a significant part in setting the pace for economic development. It is especially so with regard to blacks in American history. The paucity and inadequacy of educational facilities in addition to the courageous efforts made through various levels to provide the affected with the requisite knowledge and skills to enable them to live meaningful lives is the theme of chapter seven. In this connection higher and technical education is given special prominence in chapter eight for its relevance in economic development.

Chapter nine deals with the position of black people in self-help organizations, their agitation for a greater share of the national wealth, and their pressure for opportunities to fill their rightful place as citizens of this great country. Nothing brings this out so clearly as black protests, riots, and nonviolence movements. With the use of a few case studies, we try to understand their economic foundations and so evaluate the present level of the long and arduous journey to economic well-being in order to find appropriate measures when people play the role expected of them.

The idea for this book came from my lectures on "The Role of the Black in America and Africa" at Claremont Men's College during the fall semester of 1969. The need for such a book became clear, since there was no single textbook in the market already covering the area under study. The intellectual guidance and scientific formulation received great stimulus from Professor Harold H. McClelland, Academic Dean, and Professor W. C. Stubblebine, both of Claremont Men's College. To all these I am grateful for having given me the challenge to venture into this uncharted but bracing sea.

In the same way I am grateful to my students in this course with whom I discussed the various aspects of the question. Both sides benefited from this confrontation.

Immeasurable thanks also go to Dr. Moleti Asante, Professor of Speech and Communications, State of New York University at Buffalo, who painstakingly read through, edited, and updated the manuscript in 1974-75.

And last but not the least, my wholehearted appreciation is due to my wife, Muriel, whose searchlight eliminated many errors, and whose steadfastness encouraged me in this complex but fascinating survey.

I wish to express special thanks to Dr. Donald K. Cheek, Director of the Black Studies Center, for providing me a travel grant to visit some black educational institutions of higher learning in the spring of 1970. In a similar way, I wish to thank the Salvatori Center of the Claremont Men's College for granting me the necessary funds to cover secretarial services connected with the book. To those who read the different sections of the book and to the typists who did the excellent job of making the matter presentable, I am equally grateful. Only I am responsible, however, for any faults that remain.

MARTIN O. IJERE

SURVEY OF AFRO-AMERICAN EXPERIENCE
IN THE U.S. ECONOMY

The Study of the Economic History of Afro-Americans

The study of the economic history of Afro-Americans or that of any people for that matter should begin with some basic knowledge of the tools and techniques that are of vital importance in approaching such a study. These, for our purpose, consist in the knowledge of the nature and scope of economic history, its functions and methods and its interrelationship with other disciplines. Along with this is an explanation of the rationale in the particular study—in this case the role of blacks in American economic history, and the ways in which it is connected with the overall American economic thought.

Economic history may be defined as the study of man's efforts in the past to satisfy his material needs with the resources at his disposal. Its usefulness lies in the fact that it furnishes us with the knowledge of how to plan the future in the light of the past avoiding the pitfalls and difficulties that past generations encountered. As an intellectual discipline, economic history enables the inquirer to describe and explain the past using certain methods and techniques, to investigate the interrelationship of economic factors in development and to explore their influence on the social and political evolution of the nation. In addition to this, the knowledge of economic history enables us to establish, as far as data and other information allow, the authenticity of the past, the cause and effects of past events as well as their scientific universality.

The distinctiveness of economic history lies in the nature of the problem that it studies, namely, that of resource allocation for human consumption and satisfaction. This problem is fundamental to man and so is the discipline which investigates it, as pointed out by Heckscher:

> Economic history has a distinctly circumscribed object of its own, which cannot be fulfilled if it is constantly set aside for aims belonging to other departments of historical study.[1]

Economic history has developed many methods of scientific investigation. How and when these can be used depends on individuals and circumstances. The leading methods can be classified as *traditional, comparative,* and *quantitative.* The traditional approach is rather literary, philosophical, and empirical.[2] It synthesizes the historical and economic factors in development, the institutions and their evolution, and evaluates these in the light of available facts. In order to carry out the task of interpreting the past, the economic historian has to make conscious efforts to develop analogous experiences with the past, to understand the general background, to recognize the various interrelationships of any economic activity within its specific context, and to interpret these accordingly, giving the central issues the weight appropriate to the time period under consideration.

Two paths are then open to the economic historian: interpretation by delineating specific economic activities and concentration on the economic background of particular political and social institutions. It is this emphasis on the institutional background that has given traditional economic historians the appellation of "institutional economic historians."[3]

In another way the study must be balanced. This demands the use of the comparative method where applicable. What has happened to the black man and woman may not be unique in history. We must be able to draw an analogy between historical experiences, showing the differences and critically reexamining the evidences arrived at in the national history.

The comparative method of economic history is valuable because the economic conditions vary widely in different societies and under different conditions. The relative phenomena are selected, studied, and compared. An assessment of the processes of development within the compared areas is then postulated. This is a qualitative task that unravels the historical, social, and economic evolutions involved in a given situation. Its advantage is its universality. By the comparative method the so-called uniqueness of the historical experience is neutralized and a fuller and more comprehensive view of development is generally attained.[4]

The quantitative method has been used since the nineteenth century, though much emphasized in recent works by economic historians. It rests on positivism, namely, that nothing matters except it can be counted, measured, or weighed. It therefore employs statistical and mathematical methods, but because of the neecssity to narrow the bounds of investigation in order to find quantifiable subjects, it relies heavily on economic theory and economic development. The advantage of the quantitative method is that it helps to determine the contribution of partic- ular changes in economic institutions, increases in technology, and factor supplies among others. But it is to be remembered that quantified data are not economic history in themselves but are rather the external manifestations of economic change within a particular sphere. Furthermore, only the recent past, about a century of history, is documented sufficiently for the use of the quantitative method.[5]

THE RATIONALE FOR THE STUDY

Black economic history is an important area of study that, when explored, can provide understanding of various methods blacks have employed within the given environment to utilize the economic resources available. The factors affecting their activities are suitable subjects for a scientific investigation.

In another way black economic history exists as a part of the economic history of American society. It is also part of world history. Secondly, such an attempt is made only to give prominence to the study and to enable it to be investigated in all its ramifications.

And finally it can be said that the subject is all-embracing, reaching out into the economic history of Africa, Asia, Europe, and America from the beginning of modern times to the present. The lack of suitable studies, researches, and documentation in this field is an invitation to more active work, in order to correct misconceptions and to put the role of the blacks in proper perspective. The fault cannot be attributed entirely to black scholars whose past has been comfortably neglected by colonial masters from the Portuguese in the fifteenth-century to the British and the French and Portuguese, again, in the twentieth; or whose contribution to America is remembered only as planters and reapers of cotton. There is abundant material in the world today to guarantee full-scale investigation.

To understand well the Afro-American role in economic history two divisions are necessary: (1) the African background, which was decisive for his later role in the new world; and (2) his actual performance in the United States. The two will take into account the internal and external factors influencing his performance, such as the impact of Europeans and Arabs, and the political, social, religious, and psychological forces operating in his environment.

THE EMPHASIS ON THE ECONOMIC FACTOR

The selection of the economic is only a matter of convenience. History is a unity. The delimitation into the economic, political, religious, and ideological is simply to enable us to understand completely one phase of life. Economic history is a continuous process embodying the old and the new. Hence no study of the role of the black in America is complete without an inclusion of the past, which was his African heritage. If there is a discontinuity or discrepancy in this contribution, then there is a distortion of history.

Economic life is orderly, with an element of logic and organization. Thus given the same conditions the black in America can be expected to produce the same results as they did in Africa. This becomes immediately relevant to us, for example, in the consideration of slavery in Africa compared to that of America. We have therefore to reconstruct the past in the light above in order to arrive at meaningful conclusions.

Studied and given great prominence for centuries are such aspects of the black man's experience as: religion, literature, music, art, psychology, sociology, politics, and sports. These studies have made a significant contribution to human knowledge. However, from the first moment of birth till death, man's efforts are channeled largely to the satisfaction of his fundamental needs for food, shelter, and clothing. If these are lacking, all other activities will be correspondingly affected. The neglect of the economic aspect is due to a great extent to the general tendency to treat economic discussions as boring and complicated. After all economics was, until recently, regarded as the dismal science. Furthermore, studies on minority groups have not always everywhere received a great deal of attention and encouragement, as they have today. Hence, these areas have been neglected.

But how do we begin this extensive study? Attempts made to explain the blacks' contribution to the American economic development can proceed along many lines. Events can be woven around great names or their ideas that give birth to the events that can be discussed. We could of course concentrate on the movements of governments and political forces or perhaps emphasize the physical environment, the society, and the external world which can modify man's character and influence his economic possibilities.

The more usual approach is that which bears on the broader questions of human progress and social and economic development. Seligman describes this socio-economic aspect of man's existence thus:[6]

> The existence of man depends upon his ability to sustain himself; the economic life is therefore the fundamental condition of life. Since human life, however, is the life of man in society individual existence moves within the framework of the social structure and is modified by it. What the conditions are to the individual, the similar relations of production and consumption are to the community. The economic causes, therefore, must be traced in the last instance to these transformations in the structure of society which themselves condition the relations of social classes and the various manifestations of social life.

Seligman's argument is derived from that of Karl Marx: his economic interpretation of history, which simply explained, means that all social relations are intimately connected with the productive forces of society. If the modes of production are changed, he maintained, mankind will change its social relation. "The hand mill creates a society with the feudal lord: the steam mill a society with the industrial capitalist." It is this class of men, he states further, that will create principles, ideas, and categories in conformity with their social relations. Marx might have oversimplified the economic nature of man. He might have neglected the operation of free will and ethical and spiritual forces, or perhaps exaggerated. Yet, his theory of economic determinism is borne out by history and is largely the guiding principle in social and economic relations today. This is conspicuous particularly in the relationship between the advanced and the poor nations of the world.

The case for black economic history needs therefore no further elaboration. Economic considerations were foremost in the African slave trade. The black man's role in America started with his toils and labors—in building avenues of transportation and with agricultural labors in cotton fields and the rice swamps of the South. But slavery changed not only the economic but also the social relation of the South and its population. Whether the question of role is related to blacks, the planters, or the total economy, the important thing is to be able to see the various ramifications of the problem. The question is neither one of bookkeeping nor of economic profit, but rather of economic history generally.

THE TOOLS OF ANALYSIS

The economic historian finds recurring themes and regularities in the study of economic growth. He discovers the importance of economic and noneconomic factors—the changes in the quality and quantity of the factors of production—in terms of whose variables he is to explain economic growth, and the geographical, religious and philosophical factors that complete the total picture of economic growth.

By the use of sector growth models, an attempt is made to understand economic history. In this vein Rostow[7] has enunciated five "stages": the traditional society, the preconditions of take-off, the take-off, the drive to maturity, and the age of maturity. By such stages, countries are seen to follow a growth path more or less regular in nature. Another categorization is the grouping of the production sectors into primary, secondary, and tertiary industries.[8] Different theories produce different conclusions about industrial development. Recently Colin Clark[9] has advanced his three stages of growth: agriculture, manufacturing, and service. While these attempts provide us with the knowledge of the stages through which the economy passes, and thus bring out similarities among otherwise dissimilar situations, a fourth theory, that of Karl Marx,[10] gives an analysis of the processes by which the economy has evolved, namely, in the control of the society's means of production.

But to see the role of the black well, we must see it whole. Since the factors affecting man's attempt at satisfying his wants are interrelated, the social, political, religious, and psychological should not be ignored. As maintained by Woodman,[11] "the nation's No. 1 economic problem . . . was also the nation's No. 1 political problem, and . . . the nation's No. 1 social problem."

The Economic Heritage of the Black in America

2

We must research diligently the annals of time and bring back from obscurity the dormant examples of agriculture, industry and commerce, upon these the arts and sciences and make common the battleground of our heritage.

—ARTHUR A. SCHOMBURG

INTRODUCTION

Interest in the African heritage has always concerned black Americans. It was particularly strong during the antebellum period. At this time an intense cultural nationalism gripped the minds of blacks who extended it to economic nationalism. A leading nationalist of the movement was Henry Highland Garnet who in 1848 recounted before an audience of whites in Troy, New York, the achievements of ancient Africa as proof of the capability of blacks.[1] Garnet, an able orator, lamented the pillage of Africa by foreign powers, even though history bore evidence to the fact that it was once the cradle of civilization and the teacher and benefactor of Asians and Europeans. Two of its sons, Egypt and Ethiopia, established kingdoms, which were resplendent with wealth and culture. All these, in the view of Garnet, were grounds enough for the study of the African heritage.

The demand for building race pride was not limited to literature, art, and music. In the continued search for evidence of racial achievement the economic factor was not overlooked. By 1913 Arthur A. Schomburg was writing about black achievements in iron-smelting and bronzeworks when Europe was in its Dark Ages and America not yet born.[2] Carter G. Woodson, the father of black history, in a publication of 1913, also reminded the nation of the fact that

> in his native country, moreover the Negro produced in ancient times a civilization contemporaneous with that of the nations of the early Mediterranean; he influenced the cultures then cast in the crucible of time, and he taught the modern world trial by jury, music by stringed instruments, the domestication of the sheep, goat, and cow, and the use of iron by which science and initiative have remade the universe. Must we let this generation continue ignorant of these eloquent facts?[3]

In the same vein Monroe N. Work, who lived around the turn of the present century, spoke eloquently of the need to study the African heritage.[4] Work in his submission deprecated the many tactics used by whites to stamp blacks with the badge of racial inferiority. He rather marshaled evidence to prove the greatness of African kingdoms and their accomplishments. To the blacks he adressed a special message that they "should not despise the rock from which they were hewn."

Perhaps Marcus Garvey, and Booker T. Washington before him, provided the clearest example of economic nationalism. To be sure, Washington was more interested in domestic capitalism than he was in nationalism. Yet his preachments in favor of community economic development make him a singular force in black thought. It was left, however, for Marcus Garvey to articulate a plan for worldwide black economic development through nationalist ideology.

To some extent the philosophies of W.E.B. Du Bois, Whitney Young, A. Philip Randolph, Bayard Rustin, Malcolm X, and Elijah Muhammad constituted economic theories. In contemporary times the Nation of Islam, Operation Push, and its forerunner, Operation Breadbasket, and the Republic of New Africa have in common an economic doctrine.

SOURCES FOR THE STUDY OF AFRICAN HERITAGE

There are three main sources for African economic history prior to the twentieth century: oral tradition, archeological findings, and the writings of early European and Arab historians and travelers. In addition, we have in the twentieth century scholarly works drawing from these primary sources. Oral tradition is the most significant factor in the study of African history. One finds in this method lists of kings and emperors, accounts of wars and victories, the migrations of people and times of pestilences, but very little on the progress of farms and the means of exchange. It is through archeology that we get a complete picture. Various excavations in Africa have shown that blacks organized civilizations that were comparable to any other of the same time. These excavations have also led to a reinterpretation of African history and the correction of hitherto false opinions.

The works of Herodotus, Ibn Batuta, and Leo Africanus are crucial in unraveling the economic history of black Africa. Herodotus, in the second and third books of his *History,* described largely from personal experience what he knew of African life, praising agricultural and other nonagricultural activities of the people. Writing of the Egyptians in the Nile Valley, he noted that they "obtain the fruits of the land with less trouble than any other people in the world."

An African scholar, Ibn Batuta, regarded by some as the best "scientific authority" of all Arab travelers, made his African tour in the period 1325-1353. He contributed greatly to the commercial and geographical information of the areas he visited and noted the hazards of the desert and the greatness of the Mali Empire in 1352, which he regarded as stable. Finally, Leo Africanus, who traveled exclusively in the period A.D. 1506-1520, is regarded as a great and reliable authority on Africa. Historians have said that "every map, every textbook that touched on Africa for over two hundred years was indebted to him." In his *History and Description of Africa,* he gave considerable information on the influence of geography on the economic life of the people, and the high development of their agricultural habits.[5] The information furnished by Leo Africanus on the oasis, trade routes, salt mines, modes of living, and dietary habits of the people is enormous and merits careful scrutiny by those interested in the early economic history of Africa.

Thus, from the accounts of travelers and writers, we glimpse the state of economic history that, though existing in bits and pieces, still needs to be collected and reconstructed. Their accounts illustrate the blacks' forgotten or neglected achievements that were the objects of admiration by non-African nations of the time.

PROGRESS IN AGRICULTURE

The earliest known occupation of the Africans was hunting, which was practiced mostly by the inhabitants of the equatorial forest. There were also some fishermen living sedentary lives, making various tools and utensils. It was in Africa that a revolution in food production occurred in the fifth millennium in the Nile Valley. The earliest cultivators used neolithic tools—stone axes and sickles with wooden shafts. These people made pots and beads. Wheat and barley were the two crops responsible for the revolution in agriculture. By the seventh century B.C. agriculture had become an important occupation in the area south of the Sahara in Senegal and the Niger banks. Production was for local consumption and each village or clan attempted to produce much of its own furniture, utensils, farm tools, and other necessities. The mode of occupation conformed to the physical and climatic conditions of the area. Bush burning, cultivation shifting, and forest regeneration were all attempts by the people to accommodate themselves to the environmental conditions.

The high-water mark of agricultural achievement is seen in Dahomey, where this occupation rose to become an industry.[6] Agriculture was diversified and the use of division of labor was prevalent. Agricultural products provided the basis for industrial activities such as spinning, cloth weaving, calabash and weed carving, and the more formal ironworks and salt making. Markets were established in strategic locations to facilitate the exchange of agricultural and manufactured goods. Most of the labor was performed by domestic slaves, whose status differed from that of their counterparts in America in that the former could buy their freedom and were not regarded as the chattels of their masters. The blacks' ingenious agriculture and industry formed the foundations of the African kingdoms that rose and flourished in the Middle Ages. When Shakespeare in his "Ancient Pistol" glowingly spoke of Africa as:

> *A foutre for the world and worldings base!*
> *I speak of Africa and golden joys!*

he was referring to the legendary gold from Punt and Ophir, or Ghana, the Gold Coast and the Rand, one of the minerals that brought the European entrepreneurs to Africa after the commerce on African resources had ceased.

PROGRESS IN INDUSTRY

Artisanry was an important facet of the economy. From the early times, blacks had become skilled in basketry, textile weaving, pottery, woodwork, and metalurgy. The Pygmies manufactured back cloth and fiber baskets; Hottentots made clothing from textiles, skins, and furs; Ashantis became experts in weaving rugs and carpets and glazed pottery with great skill, and, at the same time, the Sudanese manufactured wooden ware, tools, and implements.

The African industrial achievements centered mainly on the use of iron and gold, two minerals that led to the growth of trade with the outside world. Africans were noted for their great facility in ironworking by the time they moved into the area west of the Niger Delta over 2,000 years ago. Iron hoes were of course essential to the Dahomean economy and were perhaps the most important products manufactured in the young country. Therefore, the blacksmiths were revered by the people as were all craftsmen who did good work. The manufacture and use of iron was not limited to these areas but was a common practice in many parts of Africa. Some authorities believe Africans, not the Hittites, were the first to use iron. Axes, knives, and saws were turned out with such simple equipment as bellows and charcoal fire.

In the southern Savanna, the Nok people used iron as far back as 200-300 B.C. At Meroe on the upper Nile, ironworking dated from 400 B.C. Iron-smelting was a highly respected occupation near Kane and the blacksmiths of Kane ranked with those of Awka in the Udi plateau. For centuries the Yorubas have had a special god of iron and blacksmiths called Ogun. Ilorin, Ekita, Elota, and many other places in Yorubaland specialized in iron. The same was true of Bamenda in the Cameroons. In West Africa the Nok iron techniques brought about the transition from wood and stone to iron. Its motifs were the forerunners of art forms that were later adapted to terra cotta and bronze media in central and southwestern Nigeria. This is seen in Benin and in Yoruba tools and arms.

Bronze-working deserves special mention for the decorative and religious purposes it served. Traces of metalworking have been found in Egypt, Nubia, Ghana, and Nigeria. In northern Nigeria, mainly in Jebba and Tada, copper and brass statues of people and animals are available or have been recently excavated. The Ife bronzes are world famous. Though first revealed to the outside world by Frobenius in 1910, they must have existed many centuries earlier. The heads were made by the *cire-perdue* (lost wax) process of metalworking. The same methods were applied in the making of iron objects.

Although earlier writers have attributed the introduction of the *cire-perdue* process to the Portuguese, later authorities are of the view that it was an indigenous African craft or at least borrowed from Egypt and Asia. The material posterity of Benin was due to its skill in arts and crafts, its bronze-casting by the *cire-perdue* method, and other bronze work such as swords and spears. Bronze objects are known to exist also in the Ibe town of Awka where highly decorative bowls of unusual shape have been found. Smaller traces have also been found in Ikom in Ogoja Province.

The importance of gold can be seen in its influence in the early states and empires of Africa like Ghana, Mali, and Songhay and also in its place in the commercial activities with Arabs and Europeans before 1900.[7] The inhabitants of Ghana were reputed for ironworking, but their rich deposits of gold in Wangara, so highly in demand by Arab traders, made it one of the earliest economically and politically viable states in Africa. Gold was exchanged for salt which was scarce at the time, and its control of this latter article of trade also gave it dominance. Taxes were paid in gold. To prevent inflation the state controlled the source and supply of gold. Ghana soon acquired a reputation for its gold. Early writers spoke of Ghana from 891 B.C. onwards as the "land of gold" and at a later period the British called the territory the Gold Coast.

Mali, which followed, extended its power by utilizing gold as a medium of exchange. This is typified in the oft-publicized pilgrimage of one of its rulers, Mensa Musa, to Mecca in 1324, when his five hundred slaves were said to carry a shaft of gold weighing six hundred pounds and his baggage camels carried eighty to one hundred pounds of gold. Mali's importance lay also in its possession and utilization of other minerals like copper, shells, salt, and metal pieces.

The Songhay empire, centered on Gao on the Niger River, derived its importance for the gold trade in the north and south of Djenne. This was also an area of great agricultural activity, particularly famous for barley, rice, cotton, and cattle. Banking and credit developed, and so did the establishment of weights and measures and goods inspection.

INTERNAL AND EXTERNAL COMMERCE

The African commercial activities have been both internal and external. The internal was limited to the countries and states in both east and west that traded with the north. The external trade took place between them and European and Asian countries. More often than not, the latter has received more attention in the hands of early writers who looked at African trade and commerce from a European standpoint. But both types of commerce were equally important and oftentimes inseparable. The greatest progress was made naturally in times and in areas with political stability and the commodities that entered into exchange reflected the mineral and agricultural potentialities of the territories as well as the use made of them and the people's ingenuity.

The early writers Herodotus, Ibn Batuta, and Leo Africanus described in their books the state of commerce existing in Africa from 300 B.C. to A.D. 1500. Herodotus spoke of the "silent trade" or dumb barter as early as the fourth century B.C. This was an ingenious method of exchanging goods like gold and salt between people who did not understand the same language and had no interpreters. Thus, the gold of Wangara outside Ghana was exchanged for salt obtainable from inside Ghana. Bevil remarks that this method was known to the Romans and the Chinese who employed it on the banks of a river in Pankhia in the first century A.D. It also existed in Ceylon in the fifth century A.D. and in Abyssinia in the sixth century.

Leo Africanus, on the other hand, noted the considerable profit made from the book trade more than any other line of business in Timbuktu. The strategic position of Ghana enabled it to exchange iron products, gold, and ivory from its territory with the salt from far North Taghaza. Ghana thus was the entrepôt for the supply and demand of medieval goods. By a skillful and intelligent exploitation of a nonlocal demand for West African gold and other products, Ghana's fortune rose to great heights. For example, it developed shrewd marketing policies of controlling the supply of gold to prevent inflation while at the same time limiting the extent of its intervention in the economic lives of the people by allowing the gold diggers and salt traders to carry on within the limits of their dumb barter or silent trade.

Mali traded with North Africa and carried further the developments already observed in the case of Ghana. At its height, it controlled the copper mines of Takedda, the gold fields of Bambouk and Boure, and the salt of Taghaza, in fact the major known minerals of Africa. In addition, it also controlled trade routes and cities as well as the caravan routes. The diversity of trade brought in currencies in gold, copper, shells, weights of stuffs, or in salt or metal pieces. Mali's most powerful ruler, Mensa Musa, insured the security of his travelers and traders making Timbuktu, Djenne, Wataba, Gao, and Agades great centers of trade. Annual caravans to North Africa carried thousands of pounds of gold as well as slaves, grain, and cola nuts, bringing back copper, salt, Venetian beads, and sword blades from Europe, and dates, salt and merchandise from Mighrob in the North. Mali's commercial greatness is again evidenced in the reported journey of Mensa Musa to Mecca in 1324. This trip, with the abundant gold taken along, had the effect not only of increasing the commercial position of Mali, but also of ruining the value of money in Egypt by the great amounts of gold brought in. The journey was, in turn, followed by manpower exchange and educational reforms, introduced by foreign scholars into Timbuktu.

The commercial exploits of Mali were continued by Songhay, which centered its activities around Djenne, Gao, and Timbuktu, and controlled similar products as Mali. From these cities came agricultural products like barley, rice, and cotton for the cloth and brazen vessels of Europe. Unlike Mali, which was careful to leave out religion in politics, the Songhay rulers mixed Islam and commerce in the furtherance of both, to be used as a bulwark against Christianity in later centuries. Leo Africanus described Timbuktu as a city of artificers and merchants whose growth and achievements lay in trade and tribute from conquered territories.

Much of the trading activity was intricately connected to caravans. This mode of commerce had a strong influence on African economic history. The caravans were the ancient arteries of commerce and culture between the Sudan, North Africa, and Europe. The Africans bartered gold, salt, ivory, and agricultural products, like millet and rice, for Venetian glass beads and unwrought silk. The trans-Saharan trade routes flourished for centuries and enriched the countries through which they passed, till the competition of the sea route through the Mediterranean and the abolition of the slave trade hastened their decay. The trans-Atlantic slave trade changed the direction and pattern of African commerce. As internal commerce decayed, the trade with European countries via the coast increased the African human cargoes bartered for European luxury goods.

In the discussion above we have noted the place of Africa in world history. Its role was as glorious as that of any contemporary continent or nation. Its fame drew scholars, preachers, and adventurers to it. Its wealth was so legendary that where ignorance reigned the Europeans filled it with gold and diamonds. It was in this way that mythical Prester John was clad with gold and his kingdom became the object of special expeditions into the heart of Africa.

This was the Africa whose next stage in history was clouded by the tragedy of the trade exploits in human flesh, called the slave trade. This was the Africa that was soon to become the "Dark Continent" where wealth accumulated and men decayed. The African slaves who were transported to the Americas had therefore a noble heritage economically, politically, and socially. That this heritage survives only in bits and pieces in American history shows the ferocity and the tragedy of the institution of American slavery.

Thus, early African history throws some light on the economic history of black Americans. It furnishes information on the great achievements in government, culture, and economic life that provide racial pride and point of reference for blacks in America as those elsewhere. Throughout the last century black leaders urged the study of African history, particularly the exploits of Sudanese kingdoms, Ethiopia, and Egypt.

Three early writers, Herodotus, Ibn Batuta, and Leo Africanus, have left a wealth of information on these areas. Agriculture, the basis of economic life in early Africa, nurtured one of the earliest civilizations known to mankind, namely the Egyptian. Agriculture also supported many other early kingdoms and witnessed noteworthy innovations that served a growing population and met a variety of needs.

Africa's industrial importance centers on its skilled artisanry, the use of iron and gold, bronze-working, and the *cire-perdue* method of metalworking. In the field of commerce European and Asian traders exchanged foreign manufactures and salt for African agricultural, industrial, and mineral products. Caravan routes spanned the Sahara. Africa furnished its manpower in the form of slaves to Europe before the sixteenth century and to America thereafter.

Throughout these centuries, Africans were regarded as equals by foreigners and their achievements were acknowledged. The African heritage with its lessons and its inspiration serves to underscore black activity in the United States.

3 | Black Contribution in American Agriculture

INTRODUCTION

The basic reason for the slave traffic across the Atlantic to America was economic, to meet the demand for labor created by the widening agricultural opportunities in America. There was a dearth of manpower suitable for work in the New World, and this type of manpower was to be found in Africa. Africans were said to possess the skill, stamina, and mental conditioning for working the cotton, tobacco, sugar, and rice of the South.

The story of the trade's origin, the consequences that resulted from it, and the physical and psychological experiences that accompanied it belong more to political than to economic history. But it is pertinent to mention that the African slaves were not the first labor to be tried in these areas. The explorers and colonizers had earlier experimented with the natives of the new America as laborers, but found them disinclined to work, either because of physical weakness or as a reaction to the labor exactions of their masters.[1]

Thus began the slave trade led by the Portuguese, who were later overtaken by the Spaniards, Dutch, French, and English. All engaged in the transportation of valuable African manpower for productive enterprise in the new continent of opportunities. The importance of this form of trade could be seen in many ways: the knighting of Hawkins and Drake by Queen Elizabeth I of England to whom the opening of the slave trade was a

worthy achievement; the encouragement it gave to British manufacturers—for by an Act of Parliament of 1698, "on account of the
incessant clamor of English merchants, the trade was opened
generally, and any vessel carrying the British flag was, by an act
of Parliament, permitted to engage in it on payment of a duty
of 10 percent on English goods exported to Africa."[2] Another
measure is the number of slaves transported to America: Du Bois
estimates sixty million.[3] Other writers put the figures differently.[4]
But that it was a great movement remains incontrovertible on all
sides.

From Cape Verde to the equator, and as far south as Madagas-
car, came a mixture of people: Ashantis, Moors, Malays, Ibos,
Yorubas, Dahomeans, Hausas, Mandingos, Ewes, and others—
all unwilling workers with their different languages, customs,
and habits. They were to furnish the cheap labor for "one of the
most extensive bootlegging businesses in the United States."[5]
They sustained the shipping interests of the New England states,
becoming the basis for large fortunes in the North and Middle
Atlantic states. Above all, they served as the bedrock of the plantation system.

Despite the growing literature on slavery, it is impossible to
establish exactly its economic contribution because data for such
an exercise are not generally reliable.[6] In addition, vagueness and
lack of unanimity exist as to what constitutes the gains of slavery
and the best methods of measuring its profitability.

In investigating the contribution of slavery to the American
economy, the following will be considered: organization of labor
in a plantation system and the fortunes and misfortunes of
plantations as a factor in production and productivity; the
profitability of slavery to the planters; and the effects of slavery
on agriculture, industry in particular, and the national economy
in general.

PRODUCTIVITY OF SLAVE LABOR

The plantation system and the method of labor organization
were factors in labor productivity. As a capitalistic enterprise,

the plantation system depended on heavy funding for its operations. The agricultural system was operated on the single-crop principle, although there were evidences of mixed farming. But largely the single-crop production dominated and influenced the type of labor employed. The system produced crops for external markets in the North, in England, and in Europe, and its fortunes depended on the situation in these markets. In its social set-up the plantation system was hierarchical, with the master or plantation owner at the apex and the slaves as the residuum, with the foremen or overseers as middlemen.

To reap the greatest benefit, the planters adopted two systems of work, the gang and the task. By the first the slaves were arranged in groups under a foreman whose categorical inhumanity has been chronicled through many generations. In the second case individual slaves were given specific plots of land and, although they remained still under the master's supervision, they retained some freedom to carry on their work unmolested by overseers. In some cases the task-force workers were allowed land to grow personal crops.

The greatest concentration of slavery was in cotton, tobacco, sugar, and rice plantations, respectively. Extensive supervision and division of labor were the norms in the larger plantations. Usually task workers were found in the coastal rice plantations of North Carolina and South Carolina. There was further division of labor into house servants and field workers. Two types of attitudes regarding slavery developed among slaves depending, in part, on how near they were to the master.

The efficiency of the slaves was affected by the lack of security and by other conditions under which they worked. Being regarded as property, they had no legal status and no cognizance was taken of their human personalities and rights. Their number was so abundant that scarcities were easily replenished. There was little or no regard to providing the necessary labor conditions suitable to raise productivity. Most records indicate that incentives like occasional gifts, bonuses, and prizes, which could be cited, were the exception rather than the rule. Further, the working day was unusually rigorous from sunup to sundown, seven days a week. Children were also employable to augment the labor force and to satisfy new demands.

Unionization of workers by which a slave could express his grievances or seek an improvement of his working conditions was out of the question. Unemployment did not exist but worker dissatisfaction was rampant. As a consequence certain alternative practices such as riots, insurrections, disobedience, and truancy were adopted by these forced laborers to achieve the same end. A saying developed among the field workers, "You better learn how to work work or else work will work you," to suggest slow downs.

Slave labor being involuntary, the result was sabotage and working below capacity. One notes the reaction of slaves in Maryland who in 1742 burned tobacco, houses, and residences of white masters, and stole rum, tobacco, meat, and other items of great value.[7] The slave masters answered the insurrections and the various forms of insubordination by the enactment of fugitive laws, death, branding, whipping, and the importation of white servants to check black servants who were domestic workers.

The type of education given to the slaves contributed to low performance. Most of them were kept perpetually ignorant and illiterate to prevent insolence toward their owners, which could occur if they came into contact with the ideas of liberty and freedom. Lack of education meant lack of skills and very little development of intellectual faculties. In the few cases where masters made attempts to educate slaves, they met the cynicism of their slaveholding neighbors.

Poor whites, who were in competition with slaves, opposed the training of slaves because it would conceivably increase black efficiency. Others argued that the African was basically ineducable. There were a minority who favored education as it would bring the usual influences that tend to nourish moral nature. The objective was the same in either case, to keep the African a "good" slave.

Poor whites and blacks derided each other and were used by the slaveholders to thwart any collective action by the other. In essence the poor white envied the slave's security and hated him for his material advantages, while the slave envied the white man's freedom and hated him for the advantages of his color. The poor white wage earner was pushed out of the economy with no security, and he developed a hostility that ripened into racial hatred for the black workers.

Out of the compulsive nature of slave labor arose numerous complaints that later developed into the doctrine of racial differences. Tillinghast characterized the slaves as "the very antithesis of the strenously energetic, ingenuous, and thrifty American."[8] Others maintained that they were wasteful, indifferent, generally incompetent and childlike and thus could only be driven to higher productivity by the severity of punishment. But neither brutality nor the camouflage of racism was capable of achieving the desired result. The answer lay in the fact that slave labor in itself was forced labor and, according to Adam Smith, by its very nature "indifferent and lacking in zest, frugality, and inventiveness."[9] The cruelty of the slave masters or overseers bred antagonism and reduction in the strength of the slaves and thus of output.

What diversity existed in occupations was usually found in the skilled category. To this group belonged the mechanics, masons, and carpenters who lived mostly in the towns. Others were tailors, shoemakers, cabinetmakers, painters, plasterers, seamstresses, and barbers. Such people were considered more valuable than their unskilled brothers and sisters, thus indicating that the artisan class with skills was an asset rather than a liability to a slave owner. Various advertisements of "Negroes for sale" or of runaways who were described as excellent mechanics and adroit masons were evidence of the value of skilled slaves. Because of skills they were frequently able to displace the poor white wage earners.

Slaves were to be found in large numbers in the mills, iron furnaces, and tobacco factories of Virginia. They operated the textile factories of South Carolina, Florida, Alabama, Mississippi, and Georgia. In the saltworks of Clay County, Kentucky, and the iron and lead mines of Caldwell and Crittenden counties, slaves formed the lifeblood of the industrial machine. In addition, slaves were also abundant in the railroads and other construction works. As dock workers loading and unloading boats at New Orleans, Savannah, Charleston, and Norfolk, they kept the United States active as an exporter. Some rose to become engineers at this early stage. Henry Blair invented two corn harvesters in 1836, while Benjamin Montgomery invented a boat propeller. But neither of these men, for legal reasons, was given the right of ownership over his invention.

In short, slaves were not only agricultural workers, but traditional servants, casual laborers, artisans, and mechanics. Others worked in heavy, dirty industries, such as coal mining, iron and steel, tobacco processing, and fertilizers. As dexterous mechanics they left their mark on the "historically important architecture of the old South—the ironwork in the old French section of New Orleans, the fine old residences of Charleston, the impressive buildings throughout the rural South which symbolize the plantation system—stands as a monument to the dexterity which the Negro slave quickly developed in the building trades."[10]

Melden testifies that the African's labor helped to build cities, level forests, bridge streams, tunnel mountains, lay railroads, grade highways, mine coal and iron, dig canals, quarry marble and granite, saw lumber, and in numerous ways augment the development of the material civilization of the United States.[11]

Among the slaves who were given positions of "responsibility" were the so-called drivers. These were fellow slaves with delegated authority in the absence of their masters or the official overseers to force the other slaves to work harder. Consequently, they were regarded as traitors by their fellow slaves.

The productivity of the slaves was affected equally by the nature of housing and medical facilities as by the organization of labor. The poor, squalid, unsanitary housing of the slaves of the last two centuries finds itself in the segregated, substandard housing of the contemporary ghetto. In the slave era the typical housing was the windowless, ramshackle, dilapidated cabins, with hardly any furniture or heating. These cabins, according to Stampp, were cramped, crudely built, scantily furnished, unpainted and dirty.[12] In the majority of cases slaves were crowded into small huts whose capacity was further reduced by increase in the slave population. Medical services for slaves were unheard of and the sick and infirm became the unfortunate victims of the slave system. Meals were scanty and most laborers seldom tasted fresh meat, milk, eggs, or fruits. That housing and health affected the productivity of the slaves appeared to have been ignored or treated with indifference by slaveholders. They either minimized their importance by arguing that the slaves deserved nothing better or that their masters were in no better circumstances. Even though the slaveholders could replenish the supply at will, the loss in terms of monetary income, as well as the resulting crime, delinquency, and fatalism stemming from the deficiency, cannot be overlooked.

Only in recent times have social scientists attempted to quantitatively demonstrate the effect of good housing, health, and education on the general productivity of the worker.[13] From this new discovery, which takes noneconomic factors into consideration, we can better appreciate the performance of Africans in an American context.

PROFITABILITY OF SLAVE LABOR

The aim of slave labor was the creation of utilities for the slaveholding class. These utilities, for what they were worth, were generally measured in financial returns. It is a mistake, however, to think of profitability too narrowly in financial terms. There were, of course, other advantages of owning slaves that are not measurable in monetary terms.

The nonfinancial benefits relate to unpaid domestic services as well as proceeds from food products. In the United States the main revenue came from the sale of slaves, which was dependent on the state of the British and the northern markets. Slave breeding was practiced to procure laborers for fertile agricultural areas because excessive speculation caused overproduction in crops such as cotton. Plantation self-sufficiency meant that the plantation owners had to seek distant markets.

Owing to size, large labor force, and capitalization, the slaveholding farmers were often able to outbid nonslaveholding farmers. Where conditions favored commercial production of staples, the small farmers found themselves unable to resist the competitive power of slave labor under the plantation system. This, in time, led to a process of geographic specialization, which negates the argument held by some that the success of slave owners was indicative of the competitive superiority of slave labor per se.[14]

Another lucrative source of income was the practice of renting slaves. Rented slaves were mostly skilled artisans who worked outside of agriculture. The rentals on slaves rose from $100 per slave in 1800 to $150 in 1860. These figures were higher than what planters would have earned in possible alternate areas of investment.

Slavery, as we have seen, was profitable. Hidden profits included services from household slaves, food and other provisions grown on the owner's plantation, appreciation in the value of land due to improvements, and natural increase in slaves. When these are added to the income from the sale of the staple, they increased profits for slave owners. The sale of the staple itself showed profit as the following table illustrates:[15]

TABLE 1

Annual Outlay		Annual Return	
1. Interest on capital invested in slaves (£50)	£2.10	1. Two hogheads tobacco	£16.00
2. Interest on farm capital required per slave	£2.00	2. Corn, etc.	£4.00
3. Living expenses of slave	£3.00		
Total	£7.10	Total	£20.00

From an investment of about £100, the cost per slave was £7.10 and the return was £20 or 20 percent profit on the capital investment, less the sum necessary to replace the fund.

The cost of a slave included amortization of capital, cost of supervision, food, clothing, medicine, interest charges, taxes, wages for overseers, and the actual slave purchases. Other expenditures were connected with land investment, agricultural implements, and livestock, though these were not peculiar to slave labor. Further cost was incurred by those slaveholders who purchased insurance policies where they employed slaves in dangerous tasks. Where this was not applicable, the slave holders assumed the risks themselves. There appeared to be lower costs in large plantations where the expenses for food, clothing, and medicine were kept at a minimum.

There has been no adequate formula for measuring the relationship between slave costs and productivity and thence with profitability. In making a proper estimate, account should be made of such variables as price fluctuations at a particular time, the speculation nature of the market for slaves, the location of the plantations, the tendency to increase the supply of slaves through reproduction of "smuggling" in bad times, and the unreliability of the statistics of the time. It has been claimed, however, that returns were primarily in the range of 4 to 8 percent for males and 8 percent for females, although female productivity was half to a third of male.[16] Elliot's calculation for cotton, tobacco, rice, sugar, and molasses for 1780-1853, due to slave labor, was $271,641,644.[17]

EFFECTS OF SLAVE LABOR ON AGRICULTURE AND INDUSTRY

Black contribution to American agriculture has been obscured by the controversy over the causes of Southern poverty. Some blame it on the plantation system, while others lay it on the shoulders of labor itself. Instead of apportioning blame, it would be advisable to note the defects of both and to show the overall effect on the economy.

A monoculture, as was the plantation system, led to excessive cultivation and the consequent exhaustion of the soil. Because liquid capital was hard to obtain, and the knowledge of scientific farming was crude, there was little attempt to improve the quality of the soil. Another limiting factor was the abundance of land that made the preservation of the fertility of the soil of secondary importance. The planters were preoccupied with raising the staple crops that caused the neglect of livestock and food crop production. As a result of this practice, the South imported meat and foodstuffs that it could have produced itself.

Plantation slavery was blamed also for hindering large-scale manufacturers in the South. The primary reason usually cited was the planters' fear for urban life, whereby the slaves could become demoralized with partial freedom. Another was the capital drain, in which Northerners tapped the wealth of the South through businesses they established. While it is doubtful that without slavery the South could have been any richer than it was, it is necessary to demonstrate the economic contribution of black workers as seen through their production.

The growth of the southern economy rested on slavery. "Before the Civil War," maintains Melden, "slave labor was the foundation of wealth in the South. Its semifeudal civilization could not have existed without the patient, silent toiler on the great plantations. If cotton was king, its domain rested upon the swarthy shoulders of this black Atlas."[18] This statement was typical of the views of the slaveholders themselves. It is not surprising that many of them saw its beneficial effects and thus waged a relentless war against those who opposed the system. Elliot remarks on its overall advantages:

> Slavery is not an isolated system but is so mingled with the business of the world that it derives facilities from the most innocent transaction. Capital and labor in Europe and America are largely employed in the manufacture of cotton. These goods, to a great extent, may be seen freighting every vessel from Christian nations that traverses the seas of the globe and filling the warehouses and shelves of the merchants over two-thirds of the world. By the industry, skill, and enterprise employed in the manufacture of cotton, mankind are better clothed; their comfort better promoted, general interest more highly stimulated, commerce more widely extended, and civilization more rapidly advanced than in any preceding age.[19]

He went further to say that nine-tenths of the cotton consumed in the Christian world was the product of slave labor in the United States, and that it was this monopoly that gave to

slavery its commercial value. The slaves themselves were not
partakers in the comforts their labor gave to the world. Furthermore, this value was enhanced by the invention of the cotton
gin credited to Eli Whitney in 1793. The effects of the invention
were tremendous. This is indicated by Macaulay: "What Peter
the Great did to make Russia dominant, Eli Whitney's cotton gin
has more than equalled in its relation to the power and progress
of the United States."[20] The immediate effect of the invention
was to revive the slavery system, which had received a severe jolt
at the War of Independence. Sea-island cotton was introduced
and the business prospered with the new machine. Cotton soon
became the single largest commercial crop of the South and the
largest single export of the nation. In 1790, production was 7,000
bales and by 1860 this figure jumped to 3,841,416 bales.[21] In
weight 55,000 pounds of cotton were produced in 1802, and in
1860 it was as much as 2.2 billion pounds. By 1860, cotton reached
57 percent of the total exports of the United States with a value
of over $300 million. The South depended almost entirely on
cotton and began the intensive "mining" of the soil by the
exploitation of land and labor, primarily, with a minimum use
of capital.

The high demand for cotton in English markets and the
decline of the old sources of cotton supply, notably the Mediterranean region and the West Indies, increased the prospects and
revenue of the South. Cotton culture spread between 1793 to
1860 from South Carolina and Georgia to Virginia, Tennessee,
Alabama, Mississippi, and Texas. Within a few decades after the
invention of the gin, cotton states were producing over three-
fourths of the cotton sold in the world market.[22]

Since land was abundant, planters employed more slave labor.
This was kept at a relatively low cost since few tools and little
equipment were needed to cultivate cotton. Slaves were com-
pactly massed to raise cotton rather than staples since a laborer
could only work five to ten acres. The fact that the South was
warm meant that little expenditure was incurred on slaves for
fuel, shelter, and clothing.

The slave trade grew again and thousands of slaves were

imported into America at rising prices. To obtain more wealth, planters invested their capital all the more in slaves. Cotton became the South's best money crop. The health of the cotton industry was dependent on African slaves. Thomas Dew puts this in glowing terms: "It is in truth, the slave labor in Virginia which gives value to her soil and her habitations; eject from the state the whole slave population and we risk nothing in the prediction that—the Old Dominion will be a waste howling wilderness."[23]

The same could be said of the other states engaged in the trade. These states already began by 1798 to repeal the emancipation laws that they had enacted during the War of Independence. Maryland, Kentucky, Missouri, and Virginia were slave-exporting states; while Texas, Florida, and Arkansas were importing slaves. The demand for slaves in the South was always greater than the supply.

The world price of cotton declined to 61 percent in 1815-1849 as did that of slaves. It rose to 188 percent by 1865 as did the slaves once again. Planters' interests centered on high profits through maximum application of human energy in production at a minimum expense. The slave owners who suffered fluctuations as a result of disruptions compensated themselves by the economic rent resulting from the special fertility of their land.

The economic contribution of slave labor was not limited to the South. Its influence in the North was equally great. First it offered possibilities for capital investment from the North to the South. Northerners set up businesses in the South and advanced credit to the planters through their own merchants and banks. In time they controlled the flow of the basic resources of the South making it dependent on the former for its livelihood. The northern economy expanded as a result of the real income from the slave system. Thus, the economics of both North and South became integrated with the slave system.

The South purchased the manufactures of the North: china, mirrors, silks, Bibles, books, brooms, shoes, hats, handkerchiefs, furniture, and machinery among other luxuries. The drain on southern capital and its economic exploitation has been epitomized by Woodman: "Instead of keeping our money in circulation at home, by patronizing our own mechanics, manufacturers and laborers, we send it all to the North, and there it remains; it never falls into our hands again."[24]

Slave labor enabled the South to evolve into a leisure class with land-ownership as a base and a characteristic social and political system. By its very nature it lived on the backs of the slaves, farming the plantations to the point of exhaustion without the readiness of knowledge to replenish their fertility. The slaveholding leisure class, true to form, opposed any innovations or changes in its life's pattern. Urbanization and manufacturers were frowned upon lest they would jeopardize its social and economic status. More so was the case with transportation and railroads that were feared and whose introduction was opposed in the legislature for the fear that they would bring unwanted immigrants and new ideas into the South.

There was no psychology of thrift. Conspicuous consumption prevailed, and magnificent edifices and a large number of slaves became signs of social prestige. Instead of investing in business, planters tended to invest in more slaves. Slave labor freed the leisure class from manual work and gave it the opportunity to develop superficial social graces as Southerners aped the classical eras.

When the plantation system collapsed, the cause was due less to slave labor as to many factors surrounding the system. Soil exhaustion was one decisive factor, and the lack of capital to purchase fertilizers was another. Crop diversification was difficult under the plantation system, hence planters were at the mercy of the fluctuations in distant markets. Then came the high cost of maintaining slaves, the general lack of credit facilities, and the inability of the South to change to new situations. These, coupled with the competition from the North and the rising antagonism against slaveholding and slave expansion struck the death knell to the plantation system. Its decay, however, did not completely rid the monstrous burden from our fathers' backs. They had participated in its destruction in multitudinous ways, undermining its efficiency and attacking its hypocrisy.

4 | Agricultural Transformations

FROM SLAVERY TO THE GREAT DEPRESSION

In establishing the contribution of slave labor to the American economy, it will be worthwhile to consider tenancy and share-cropping which with crop lien placed a penalty on efficiency and built the South again to its prewar status of economic subordination. In the case of tenancy, we shall compare the system with that found in Africa under slavery and assess why the results obtained differed.

The colonial land system in America was primarily of the large plantation type with its capitalistic nature, usually employing unfree laborers under a united direction and control, and engaging in monoculture. There was a plantation owner who, in addition to capital, owned land, labor and equipment. His labor supply was inexhaustible and financially inexpensive, and he employed all means to maximize its use. By the engagement of overseers, the planters controlled labor, which was organized in gangs or given task work assignments. Cotton and tobacco were the main crops and their cultivation, without due regard to replenish the fertility of the soil, led to soil exhaustion. It was, of course, not only monoculture, or the institution of slavery, or the nature of the planters that brought about the soil deterioration; rather, it was such factors as physical surroundings, markets, government regulations, and low profits that limited improvements.[1]

The land system affected productivity in another way. The excessive emphasis on profits to the disregard of the health of the slaves meant greater output of export crops and lesser output of good livestock. Insufficient diets were the result of neglect and the lack of meat. There were few work animals on the plantation, and those that happened to be available were unhealthy and weak. Although southern planters blamed these deficiencies on the condition of the land and the climate, recent studies have demonstrated that the contention was not correct. Eugene Genovese says "in 1868 Lewis F. Allen, in his study of American cattle, said bluntly that the soil and climate of the South were fine for animals and that expressions to the contrary were little more than excuses by planters who preferred to raise cotton."[2]

The conditions under which the slave worked were subhuman and could not induce efficient labor. His work habits were unenthusiastic and as his culture and dignity were undermined, his productivity suffered even more. The problem lay in the character of forced labor. Of particular relevance now is the fact that the slaves had neither security of tenure nor that of person. They could not own land, nor could they buy their freedom.

A comparison with African land tenure system brings the differences with the American pattern into proper relief. In Africa, land is communally owned and shared by the chief or family head. Neither of them has the power of life and death over their subjects or subordinates. Communal spirit and personal relationships govern the alienation of land. In effect, land cannot be bought or sold, but remains the sole property of the inhabitants. It is the heritage from the ancestors to the living, for use by the living, and for safekeeping for future generations. Each member of the community, arranged in kindreds or extended families, can acquire an interest in the land, and these interests can mature into legal rights.

Slaves can acquire these rights and may still retain it even though the status of slavery has long been abolished.[3] Of the Nupe slaves in Nigeria, Nadel observes that

custom even guaranteed the slaves a not inconsiderable measure
of economic and social independence. An adult male slave would
work for his master in the same way as sons and junior relations
work for the head of the household. If he was put to farm work,
he would be given a small plot of his own to cultivate in his spare
time. Or if he helped his master in a craft or in trade, he would
be able to count on a regular commission. . . . In wars, they would
have their share of the booty. Slaves thus could acquire property,
and the more fortunate owned horses, sheep, cattle, money—even
slaves of their own.[4]

In contrast to the American system, the African slave retained
his economic and personal rights to own his plot of land and to
build a family. His freedom was limited in so far as he had to
give a greater share of his labor to the master, but the extent to
which the latter could encroach on the former's personal rights
was limited by local customs and rules on personal property.
Slaves were in reality more for social status than as an economic
asset.[5]

In the African land tenure system, the slaves lived with the
people and were not regarded as inferior at work though socially
they were a step down the ladder. They could buy their freedom
and rise to be slave owners themselves. They had the right not
only to acquire land, but to possess the products of their labor.
In the area of health, they were well cared for, and well housed.
Speaking of the Royal Estates in Nigeria, Meek noted that on
each of these estates, "there is a small hamlet where in former
times, the royal slaves lived and worked—providing the king with
produce; the king in turn providing the slaves with food and
clothing and a plot of land for their own use."[6] Oftentimes, they
were richer than the nonslaves, since they were allowed certain
freedoms and offered bonuses especially in the case of those whose
slave status was due to their being offered as hostages to the local
gods. These were given the best cultivable land and good livestock, and they performed the annual rituals in which animals
were slaughtered, which in the end were consumed by them.

In effect, the African slave was recognized as a human being.
His slave status was in some cases advantageous, economically and

educationally. In the early twentieth century, the slave children were the first to be sent to the white man's school before even the children of their masters. From the thirteenth century to the eigheenth, we have cases of African slaves like Jaja of Opobo rising to be a great entrepreneur in the oil trade in the Bight of Biafra. Jaja was bought in an Ibo slave market at the age of twelve and taken to Bonny, where his ability soon enabled him to acquire wealth and influence, and he became a serious rival to the chief of Bonny and later to the British oil traders.[7]

Slavery as an institution was not a vital part of African economy, but rather incidental to it. The productivity of the slave worker did not differ in any degree from that of other nonslaves. Rather, he often had a greater incentive and was able to express his ability in amassing wealth.

A comparison of the characteristics of slave labor under African and American systems is a safe guide to a reasonable estimate of their effects and for the appreciation of the differences in their productivity. The African system allowed the slave some dignity and pride in himself and his work, whereas the American system stripped him of these. The African slave was a functioning part of the land system in which he participated unlike the American situation. The reactions of both groups to their environment were consequently different. The African land tenure system was one of life; but the American was that of slavery.

The American emancipation of slaves in 1863 brought with it drastic changes in the structure of the Southern economy. The plantations began to lose their slave hands to the cities. The plantation owners employed paid labor, but the attempt with the former slaves seldom proved successful. Unfortunately, the poor whites were not forthcoming to take their places, because they would not work side-by-side with blacks. Nor was their number large enough to supply the cotton plantations with the needed labor. The wage system was thus abandoned after a few years of trial and new methods of production were tried.

Many of the planters sold their plantations, abandoning farming altogether. Within a short time the New South had a growing quantity of small farms run by individual proprietors. The freed slaves could participate in this movement toward peasant proprietorship. Their former masters oftentimes encouraged them to buy land that they had divided into small strips for sale on the installment plan. Yet only a few blacks succeeded in meeting the annual payments and becoming the owners of the land they cultivated. Only about five percent of the freed men were reported to have become owners of land in the cotton belt by 1876.[8] Furthermore, those who did purchase land frequently saw it taken from them by unscrupulous lawyers and courts.

The failure of the wage system brought in the sharecropping system, whereby the plantations were divided into allotments of from fifteen to forty acres each. Each allotment was cultivated by a share tenant or sharecropper. The difference between both lay in the fact that the share tenant had a greater degree of independence, owning his own capital and making part of the investment in the business. He may have paid cash rent for the land with a fixed amount of the product. Sometimes rent was paid in kind, either a fourth or third of the crop. Invariably he obtained his advances from the landowner. He also had a lease on his land with the possibility of renewal, whereas the sharecropper had no such rights. The latter's duty was to cultivate a crop of a certain kind, receiving a fraction at the end of the year.

It was as sharecroppers that most of the Negroes earned their living after the emancipation. The system put them completely in the hands of the landowner, whose overriding aim was to provide bare subsistence for the croppers. But the worker had less security of continuous subsistence under sharecropping than had the slave. He was saddled with debt to the landowner and was dependent on him for the type of goods he could buy. For it was the landowner who owned the country store and fixed the prices. In addition, his interest rates for money lent were as high as 10 percent for the few months from planting to harvest time. This equaled some 30 to 60 percent per annum. The nature of the crop itself was to the disadvantage of the sharecropper. Cotton was a fluctuating industry and at this time a declining one. From 1875 to 1895, it declined in price from 11.1 cents a pound to 5.8 cents a pound. The sharecropper was faced with constant erosions like the one of 1875 when more than 30 percent of the cotton land eroded beyond repair. He lacked the education to adopt methods to counter the erosion; thus the arable land available to him was depleted. Crop rotation was not practiced. It was only in the 1870s that fertilizer was introduced and this compensated for the shortage in land and other wastes. There were other handicaps with cotton cultivation, its being an exhaustive feeder and its being easily damaged by drought and heavy rain.

But the cropper had to continue to grow cotton, since it was all that the country store would accept as payment for the "advances" made by the landowner. It was also the only acceptable crop with market prospects for the landlords. As a nonperishable crop it could survive the arduous journey on the South's primitive road and rail system. The sharecropper could not grow and sell another crop. In fact, he could not sell his portion of the crop until he had paid all debts to the landlord.

Accumulation of debts forced some sharecroppers to leave the farms. But this was a risky venture because finding work in the immediate area was difficult due to agreements between landlords and landlord-merchants to refuse to hire any one who had deserted his landlord. Wages were by no means better and the share of the crops was usually the same. The white planters penalized and ostracized any of their members who broke with this system, thus the wandering unemployed black was faced with the possibility of arrest for "vagrancy" and fined. Since in most cases he could not pay, he was given over to the landlord who paid it. The "vagrant" worked for the landlord till the debt was repaid. Slavery had been reinstituted. The cropper became a wage earner who owned nothing but debts. If he continued to escape, he was turned over to the courts for breach of contract, and the former wage earner found himself working in a prison camp for a turpentine baron or in the mines or rice fields. These practices produced cultural distortions within the black community. Blacks found themselves in this condition due to lack of federal support.

The failure of the Radical Reconstruction Program, to allot "forty acres and a mule to every freedman"[9] did not allow the redistribution of private lands. Redistribution was opposed by liberals of both North and South. Credit was also hard to obtain, and those who had it were refused sales by the plantation owners. The Southern liberals preferred a system of wage laborers instead.

Many freedmen refused to work for whites during the period from 1868 to 1878, hoping that land would eventually be re-divided from the Freedmen's Bureau or some other government agency. The white leaders in the South, to squelch this hope, bought up all vacant or abandoned land available to prevent any federal redivision. This process was essentially complete by 1869. The Freedmen's Bank failed as land was not available to blacks and the wage contract system emerged to the delight of the southern leaders, who also saw in it a license to revive slavery on their plantations with numerous restrictions on the actions and personal behavior of the freedmen workers. In the wage contract the type, amount, and quality of work expected were carefully set out. Absences were fined at fifty cents a day, with no exception made for illness. The workers could not leave the plantations in the daylight without permission, and workers were expected to be quiet in their houses at night. This wage labor system was the prime source of black employment up to 1880.

In the next decade, a large number of farm hands migrated to the cities in the South where demand for menial labor was significant. The exodus left the South without some of its most skilled employees. Those remaining behind bought farm implements and equipment and rented land. The less well off were able to rent the land and the equipment from the planter and the local store.

A Bureau of the Census survey of 1930 showed five categories of southern farmers among blacks. There were landowners (13 percent), cash tenants (7 percent), share tenants (15 percent), croppers (28 percent), and wage laborers (37 percent). The general condition of all of them except the landowners was still precarious with many suffering from malnutrition and all manner of diseases. Furthermore, they could not participate in the money economy, and the credit doors were generally closed to them.

There was little incentive to improve crop production in the face of wild fluctuations in prices and constant danger of erosion. With the adoption of the sharecrop system by the South, "the credit-single-staple-tenancy-erosion cycle operated to produce poverty for most and economic insecurity for all. . . . The Great Depression that hit the nation in 1929 was nothing new to the farmers of Dixie, for most of them had known little other than hard times." The black thus became an unwilling victim of a system in many ways as bad as slavery.

TRANSFORMATIONS SINCE 1930

The changes in southern agriculture in the past decades are not only related to agricultural activities and attitudes but are also part of the total societal transformations. To understand the situation of blacks today in agriculture, it is necessary to discuss changes in life-styles. Furthermore, changes in racial attitudes have helped redefine the political and social position of blacks. Perhaps most important, the rapid urbanization that has been occurring in the United States had profoundly affected the agricultural life of all Southerners, and especially black Southerners.

Africans legally emerged, of course, from the institution of slavery at the conclusion of the Civil War. However, while according to the law blacks were free, in actual fact freedom was nonexistent. Several factors combined to keep things disturbingly similar to slavery. Unprepared for any occupation other than farm laborer, the black person remained largely dependent upon his former master in a manner strikingly similar to slavery.[10] Furthermore, through local agreements among landowners he was at the Southerners' mercy. Life was uncertain and many blacks concluded that it did not pay to put a lot of trust in their economic future. There are numerous instances in which legislative action was taken to make such coercion of the black easier to accomplish.[11]

The system under which southern agriculture operated from the time of the Civil War until the early twentieth century created an unfavorable position. It was not until the first decades of this century that major changes beneficial to the black citizen took place. Racism and discrimination were so ingrained in the political processes of the nation that Congress itself was immobilized.

This early condition has been remedied somewhat in the last few decades as the life-style of the South has changed. For one thing, the farm population is more mobile now and the sharecropper system no longer has the power it once had.

However, while the worst of the sharecropper system has been eliminated, it is nearly impossible for most blacks to own their own land, for now it takes $15,000 to $20,000 to enter southern agriculture. This means that black landownership has not increased very fast even in recent years. In fact, in the first half of the twentieth century, black ownership and occupancy actually declined drastically.[12] One reason for this is that blacks were leaving the farm. However, those blacks remaining on the farms were cultivating more land and were more competitive with the larger farmers in the bargaining for the sale of their crops.

One development that has changed agriculture is the revolution in agricultural technology. In the United States, agriculture has moved from an individualized, highly laborer-oriented enterprise to a capital-intensive, highly commercialized one.[13] Basically, the substitution of capital and technology for labor has resulted in an increase in productivity measured in output per manhour.

Machinery has been an important addition in recent years. Pesticides, fertilizers, and other chemical treatments have aided greatly, as have more advanced scientific methods of crop rotation, planting, and harvesting. Through utilization of technology, output per acre has increased. Since the 1930s, this increase in laborsaving devices has led to a doubling of the size of farms. Now there are fewer farmers needed to produce the same amount of food as before. Thus, the small farms are dwindling in number, and larger, more efficient ones are becoming the major sources of farm products now.

This can be contrasted to the old method, dying rapidly but not yet dead, that the black sharecropper or wage hand has used for one hundred years. Row-crop farming, as it is called, was primarily a seasonal type of farming. Using mules the average farmer can cultivate about twenty-five acres. This type of farmer is finding it increasingly difficult to compete with the larger, more efficient farmer and is being largely pushed out. Only in those instances where blacks have organized into cooperatives have they been able to survive.

Racial attitudes and race relations have had an important bearing on southern agriculture as well as throughout American society. The poor black farmers in the South are no longer totally subservient to white society, and they are challenging the old, racist methods of "keeping the black man in his place." With the aid of such legislation as the Voting Rights Act of 1965, the black became a political force in the Old South. The ordinary black citizen is gradually being assimilated into the American mainstream. Although this process is slower in the South than in any other part of the United States, these changes are occurring in the South as well.

Deviations from old patterns of racial prejudice and subjugation have given the black farmer a psychological feeling of independence that has changed the old pattern of subservience and fear which kept the black sharecropper and tenant in an inferior position. The black farmer, more inclined to feel the equal of his white counterpart, has been increasingly ready to compete in the agricultural market with the other producers. Perhaps the most significant single occurrence contributing to the changing situation in southern agriculture has been the migration to urban centers in both the North and South.

In 1900, blacks lived almost exclusively in the rural South, working mainly on farms. Very little migration occurred until 1910, after which several factors combined to bring about a rapid exodus of blacks from the South. The boll weevil spread throughout the Old South in the first two decades of the twentieth century, seriously disrupting the cotton industry and making cotton production difficult. This put many of the tenants out of work. The First World War increased the need for labor in the northern industrial cities. Therefore, many of the displaced black farmers moved North, as did others desiring a chance of a better life in the city.[14]

This migration was viewed with alarm by some of the southern farm owners. The idea of losing much of their cheap labor was cause for concern.

Furthermore, not all migration from the farms was to the North. Some of the blacks left the rural areas for southern cities. These cities have grown phenomenally in this century and much of their increase is properly attributed to the black ex-farmer. Since 1940 this growth has been most dramatic; the black population of southern rural areas declined 67 percent between the aforementioned date and 1960, while the number of blacks living in southern urban areas has increased 81 percent. In fact, by 1960, 72 percent of all blacks in the United States lived in urban areas.

These figures dramatically demonstrate the rapid urbanization of the black population that has occurred since 1900. At that time, a large majority of blacks lived in the rural South, while today an almost equally large majority of blacks dwell in urban areas. Without a doubt, the black's place in southern agriculture has been radically changed by the urbanization of the population. Today there is a variety of occupations. There are black independent farmers as well as sharecroppers and wage tenants. Of those remaining on the farms, an increasing proportion are becoming owners of reasonably large farms producing a diversified group of products. Those who remain in agriculture as farm hands are increasingly able.

The role of blacks in southern agriculture has changed significantly since the turn of the century. Where once the black, though theoretically free, was virtually a slave, he is now reasonably independent and able to leave the land if he desires to do so. Changes in attitude and technology have allowed land ownership and the management of larger tracts of land. The black is thus a farmer on a larger scale than previosuly, if indeed he remains a farmer. The most important story, however, is the black exodus from the institution of agriculture. The role of many blacks in agriculture has become nonexistent as they have left the rural South for the urban, industrial areas of both the North and South. Therefore, agriculture has become less important to the black population as a continually smaller percentage remains in a rural setting.

5 Black Experience in Industry

The precise date of black participation in American industry cannot be ascertained with any degree of accuracy. A variety of factors are responsible for this, chief of which is the lack of statistics on black occupations except in agriculture prior to the end of the last century. Furthermore, as slaves, blacks were not regarded as having legal rights and were not counted or classified in the regular work force. Those who worked in industry did so either surreptitiously, hiding away from the slave-owners or in defiance of them. These categories of activities, even after emancipation, were regarded as so inconspicuous that the white society hardly bothered to include them in the census enumerations of the times. Oral history and the documents on black protests provide the only sizable amount of information on blacks in industry.

There are many different components of industry.[1] Artisanry was the earliest occupation of blacks outside agirculture. Manufacturing was next as an occupation, and blacks processed basic economic commodities that had utility in black communities. The techniques used were simple since access to the knowledge of manufacturing was, in the historical experience of blacks, carefully kept away from them.

However, the bulk of them found a means of livelihood in small business, indeed the Brimmerian "Mom" and "Pop" industry, where the unit of organization was the family, the bulk of capital came from the family, and virtually all the labor was drawn from the family. Those who felt the pinch of racial discrimination most were businessmen. From Alabama to Kansas, from Mississippi to Virginia they raised their voices in protest against the lack of opportunities for them and their folks to earn a decent living in America. As we shall see in a later chapter, most of them sought to emigrate. Not all of them left the country. In fact, due to lack of finance, more than of will, the majority stayed and established the basis, even if on a modest scale, of what we call today Black Capitalism or black control of black business.

Another industrial component of great significance is allied to this, namely, the services. Retailing, undertaking, haircutting, cosmetology, and restaurants were some of the occupations that found favor and a ready market. In fact, there were many monopolies catering almost exclusively to black communities. In the wake of racial discrimination blacks were systematically excluded from the social life of the general society. Jim Crow laws and the prevailing attitude of racial superiority of whites relegated blacks to the background and made many withdraw into themselves and their communities. Since blacks could not obtain service in white restaurants for example, they had to establish their own or starve. In barbering blacks held a natural monopoly. Few whites for social and artistic reasons dared challenge their competence in doing this well. Services therefore were important even in slavery times.

The training ground for black businessmen was the school of life. Most learned by trial and error. Some had worked in mines, factories, and shipyards or acted as cooks and stewards in sailing vessels, which became their school of apprenticeship. Sooner or later these blacks decided to set up their own modest businesses.

The past is an excellent instructor for us as we seek the answer to the Afro-American's limited impact on American industry. Nevertheless we should be aware of the successful attempts at business in the face of crippling circumstances. In the next sections we shall discuss the historical development of black participation in industry, touching as much as possible the different components mentioned above. In addition we shall select two important areas of activity, namely, banking and insurance for detailed study in order to illustrate the problems that blacks faced and the successes which they attained in the development of black entrepreneurship. Having done that we shall then grapple with the concept of "Black Capitalism," discuss the arguments for and against its promotion, and note what has been achieved already, if anything, in this area. We shall reserve to another chapter a more detailed consideration of the black as worker per se. Here we shall consider him largely as self-employed.

EXPERIENCE IN DIFFERENT INDUSTRIAL SECTORS

Although agriculture was for centuries the main occupation of blacks, a trickling number of them derived their means of livelihood outside it as smiths, tailors, plasterers, painters, mechanics, and artisans.[2] Incidentally, these were occupations that served the needs of agriculture or an agricultural class. The economic and social status of the artisans was higher than that of agricultural workers, though neither was given any legal or civil rights to person and property. Slaves that had skills were worth about twice as much as those without. In an era of poor transportation some blacks carried agricultural and manufactured goods to the markets, while others herded cattle across the country, thus giving utility of time and place to these economic goods.

The earliest and greatest success of blacks in industries came in the service industries, where they could cater for specialized markets and tastes. The case of Shivers of Smithfield, Virginia, noted for his hams, is an example. This firm was able to serve cities as far away as Boston. In North Carolina, a black, Mr. W. P. Evans of Lauringburg, operated a successful store, and a Scott Bond was a successful plantation owner in Arkansas where he engaged in merchandising and brokerage. Agricultural industry developed, too, under the leadership of Huberts in Georgia, and J. G. Groves became known as "potato king" for his skill in this industry. The success of these people was due, to a great extent, to the degree of freedom allowed them in the upper South where, with the relative isolation of the blacks in their own settlements and towns, they had no inhibitions or handicaps to developing enterprise. In the lower South, on the other hand, the blacks were in a worse position through racial prejudice and limited capital, even though they outnumbered their white neighbors. Thus the integration of blacks with whites tended to squeeze out the economically weaker class.

The result of this was a steady migration of people to the North and West. In time the following cities emerged—Bassett, Cabin, Creek, Greenville, Roberts, Weaver, and Lost Creek in Indiana. Similar settlements of blacks existed also in Ohio—Long, McIntyre, and Randolph; in Michigan there was Calvin Township; in Colorado, the Deerfield; in Nebraska, the Brownlee, and in New Jersey, the Snow Hill. The settlements in the South were few: Averett in Virginia; Method in North Carolina; Baldwin in Alabama; and Des Velente, Chambers, and New Africa in Mississippi.

After the Civil War there were drastic changes in labor organization and crop production. In industry the effect was to tilt the balance already existing with agriculture. The percentage in agriculture began to decrease; 98 percent during slavery, 87 percent in 1900, 80 percent in 1910, 10 percent in 1960. In the last period there were 15 percent in domestic services, 10 percent in semi-professional and professional trades, 12 percent in retail and wholesale, 8 percent in clerical, 5 percent in construction. There has been a marked improvement in the industrial position of the blacks in times of national growth and business boom. As the national income rose from $13 billion at the end of the nineteenth century to $22 billion at the beginning of the twentieth and $40 billion by 1918, the general employment situation in America has increased, rising from twenty-seven million in 1889 to thirty-nine million in 1918. The number of blacks in manufacturing rose from 275,000 in 1900 to 693,000 in 1910, and 960,000 in 1920. While there was a decline in the number of those in domestic and personal services by about 20 percent, there was a doubling of those in trade and transportation.

World War I was a period of high employment for blacks, as new products created a demand for more labor, which could not, as in previous times, be met by the supply from Europe. Just as there were intensive recruitment drives in Europe for Germans, Irish, and Italians in the nineteenth century, there was also a similar activity in the South for black workers at this time.

It was also during World War I that the first upsurge of black activity occurred in retailing, personal services, entertainment, and real estate. Blacks concentrated on small-scale enterprises because of the dearth of credit, business connections, poor customers, and weak organization as well as a hostile dominant society. There followed correspondingly a decline in the laboring class of farm hands, some of whom had migrated to the North.

The Great Depression had disastrous effects on blacks. For example, participation in wholesale and retailing was small. Only one percent of the total retail business was black in 1930, in spite of the fact blacks made up nine percent of the American population. Even the market in black communities was controlled from the outside. No similar competition existed in semi-professional businesses like hairdressing, undertaking, barbering, and dentistry because of the nature of the services.

One of the organizations that supported participation in business was the National Negro Business League, established in 1910 by Booker T. Washington. Since its inception, its impact has been great. The number of blacks engaged in various types of business enterprises for example rose from 40,445 in 1900 to 103,881 in 1930 largely as a result of its work. Even though the ensuing Great Depression took a heavy toll of many black businesses, it caused a consolidation in some. In 1940 there were only 87,475 black businessmen according to the year's census, which was a decrease of 16 percent although the number represented an increase of 116 percent over that of 1900. Consolidation has been the norm in American industries ever since the 1940s and the number of black businesses has correspondingly declined comparatively. Major multinationals have more and more controlled the industry and business of America; blacks have been isolated from this economic power.

While specialized service industries like restaurants, barber shops, hotels, and undertaking still carry on and dominate the black market, other businesses like banks and transportation have shown marked retrogation. In some others like broadcasting, blacks are an insignificant number. By way of illustration, there were 17,500 authorized automobile dealers in the country in 1968, of whom only seven were black, and of the 6,000 radio stations only eight were black.

A look at black banks and insurance companies gives the same conclusion that things have been difficult for blacks in American business.

BUSINESS EXPERIENCE
WITH BANKING AND INSURANCE

The period 1790 to 1860 saw several attempts at banking by black businessmen who previously had invested their funds in United States securities and, in adition, made loans to their less fortunate neighbors. Their savings came from such businesses as dry goods, real estate, brokerage, and insurance, the last being the greatest lever to the banking business. Another form of encouragement came from black leaders who emphasized thrift and savings and the importance of developing the self-employed independent worker. The consensus among black leaders was that a bank would satisfy these objectives and lead to the further improvement of the blacks, especially in supplying funds for housing and retail trade and in creating more employment for them.

There were obvious difficulties to be surmounted before the above aims were realized. The first was how to provide credit for the poor. The low purchasing power and market value of property coupled with the limited liquidity of their real estate militated against the abilities of the poor to obtain loans. White financiers who supplied credit did so at exorbitant rates of interest. Nonetheless the first bank set up by whites for blacks (the Free Bank of New Orleans) opened in 1864. The Civil War saw other savings banks in Virginia and South Carolina for black soldiers. With the end of the war, a campaign for a separate banking institution for blacks was launched in many states. The result was the Freedmen's Bank, established in 1865, stipulating that

> the general business and object of the corporation hereby created shall be to receive on deposit such sums of money, as may from time to time be offered therefore by or on behalf of persons heretofore held in slavery in the U.S., or their descendants, and investing the same in stocks, bonds, treasury notes, or other securities of the United States.

Confidence in the bank was created by its being established by an Act of Congress and by its attachment to the Feedman's Bureau. It had branches in various parts of the country and drew depositors from both black and white. Departures from the original statutes included the acceptance of deposits from nonblacks, the erection of new structures to house the bank in Washington, D.C., at the cost of a quarter of a million dollars, and an amendment in the charter of the bank in 1870 permitting loans on real estate.

The beginning of the bank was beset with difficulties. Record keeping was poor and the employment policy discriminatory. Few blacks were employed in the various levels of the establishment and in fact at first hardly any at all. Notwithstanding the favorable business climate in which it was born, the large patronage, monopoly of the black population, and government supervision, mismanagement crept into the bank, creating panic among the bank's clientele and hence to a run on it.

The failure of the Freedmen's Bank was disastrous in terms of black morale as well as in its immediate financial consequences.[3] With it went loss of faith in savings banks. Booker T. Washington characterized the black mood when he wrote that "it was a long time after this before it was possible to mention a savings bank for Negroes without some reference being made to the disaster of the Freedmen's Bank."[4]

This failure however led the blacks to establish private banks of their own. The first of such banks was the Capital Savings Bank of Washington, D.C., in October, 1888. The True Reformer's Bank of Richmond, Virginia, opened to business in April, 1889. During the same year the Mutual Bank and Trust Company of Chattanooga, Tennessee, was established. The Alabama Penny Savings Bank came in 1890. Why were these beginnings possible at all? Looked at closely we see that they were established by black insurance interests. The True Reformer's Bank of Richmond, for example, was under the corporation of the Grand Fountain United Order of True Reformers, itself a fraternal society located in Richmond. The bank served as a depository for the order and became subordinated to the latter. Its failure was also largely due to incompetence in banking practices and to negligence. Another feature of early black banks is their religious connection. The various denominational churches were active in promoting banks for the economic welfare of their member. Religious ministers lent the financial institutions the expertise, integrity, and their organizational ability. Banks so connected were: The Nickel Savings Bank, depository of the People's Insurance Company in Alabama (1896); The St. Luke's Penny Savings Bank (1903), depository of the Independent Order of St. Luke; the Galilean Fisherman's Bank in Hampton, Virginia (1909), depository of the Grand United Order of the Galilean Fisherman; The Mechanics Savings Bank (1902) in Richmond, Virginia, depository of the Knights of Pythias.

According to the 1951 report of the United States Department of Commerce, fourteen banks belonged to blacks. Their total assets amounted to $32 million. Eleven of these banks were located in the South. There were in addition twenty-five savings and loan associations owned and operated by blacks. Their total assets amounted to $16 million in 1949.[5] In 1970 nearly seventy banks belonged to blacks.

The first industrial insurance companies developed from the

"benefit" societies. They paid members higher sickness and death benefits than the fraternal organizations. Life insurance dated from the eighteenth century and rested on the patronage and support of black churches. Ministers of religion, anxious to provide sickness and burial benefits to their members were quick to organize fraternal societies from which developed the modern insurance companies. Three examples of such church-connected insurance companies in Philadelphia can be cited: Crucifixion Society by the Crucifixion Church; Avery Society by the Wesley A.M.E. Church; and in Atlanta, The Helping Hand by the First Congregational Church.

The Free African Society was organized in Philadelphia in 1787 to give support to its members in sickness, child care, and for burial purposes. But the first black-owned insurance was the Philadelphia African Insurance Company, 1810, which started with a capital of $5,000. The greatest success attained by blacks so far in the insurance business is the North Carolina Mutual Life Insurance Company of Durham, North Carolina, whose president for many years was the indefatigable entrepreneur Charles Clinton Spaulding. His connection and success with this insurance are as exciting as they are encouraging to others. He rose above enormous odds. An eighth-grader, impecunious, having no business tradition, and operating in a hostile environment with nonpatronage from whites, Spaulding and his associates began with a few dollars what today has matured into a giant enterprise and a living credit to Afro-American business. Characteristic of his business acumen was his own description of his work: "When I came into the office in the morning I rolled up my sleeves and swept the place as janitor. Then I rolled down my sleeves and was an agent. And later I put on my coat and became the general manager."[6] At his death in 1952 the company's assets were worth more than $33 million, and it was reputed to be the largest Life Insurance Company in the black world. In addition to the more normal business of insurance it promotes health, education, and social welfare in the eight states where it operates.

It is not surprising that Charles C. Spaulding rose in the business world. He was the president of the National Negro Insurance Association and president of the National Negro Business League, in 1921 and 1926 respectively. Furthermore, he served as trustee of Howard University, Shaw University, and North Carolina State University.

Generally, black insurance companies have profited from the social situation in the country. Racial discrimination extended to policyholders by white insurers guaranteed the black market from white competition. While this was the case, the picture has changed somewhat since the 1950s and a greater part of the black bourgeoisie has begun to patronize white companies. White insurance companies, in their attempt to prove that they are Equal Opportunity employers, are scooping away the cream of black college graduates and are using them to penetrate the black market.

What do we learn from our historical excursion into the black experience in industry so far? First, we observe a demonstration of indomitable courage among blacks to penetrate industrial activities despite personal and social obstacles. The second lesson of the past is the degree of failure accentuated in recent times by ghetto isolation and white attitudes.

Black entrepreneurship developed long before Marcus Garvey began his frontal attack on the lack of opportunities for blacks in business at the beginning of the century. But it was he above others who gave the greatest encouragement to black ownership and management of business. Ideologically Garvey was a capitalist but he provided blacks with a demonstration of entrepreneurship that could be used for social purposes.

What then does the future hold for blacks in industry? In the last five years the market has been bombarded with treatises on black businesses. There have emerged such journals as *Black Enterprise, Business Management,* and *Back Economic Development,* to name a few. In addition the *Harvard Business Review* and *Business Week* are among the white journals that are devoting their columns to black business histories. Such discussions as are occurring in various circles suggest that blacks will find capitalism to be a valuable tool for community development. While this is one possibility, which we will explore, alternative answers may be needed to solve pressing social needs.

BLACK CAPITALISM: A DELUSION?

A study in 1967 by the Cabinet Committee on Price Stability reported that major companies were merging throughout the business field. By 1967 the 100 largest manufacturing corporations held about the same share of assets (of all corporations combined) held by the 200 largest in 1948. The 78 corporations with assets of $1 billion or more held 43 percent of the total assets. The 1,320 corporations with assets of $25 million or more than, 0.7 percent of all manufacturing corporations, held 82 percent of the total assets. In 1967 there were aproximately 186,320 manufacturing corporations in the U.S. according to the Cabinet study. In 1968 only 781 or 0.42 percent or about 4 companies in every 10,000 received 49 percent of all manufacturing profits. It is therefore clear that blacks competing in the business field will never achieve a fair share of the fruits of capitalism. There would have to be an economic revolution before those left so far out of the sharing of capital could have an equal chance.

Some blacks have espoused a sort of "black capitalism," which to them means the ownership and management of economic enterprises by blacks as necessary for personal independence and racial pride. They urge black participation in the industrial life of the nation. To them the many advantages offered by industry must be open to the blacks, that is, the provision of employment for increasing populations, the fullest utilization of those who are underemployed, the raising of living standards by an increase in per capita income, and the creation of racial prestige.

Blacks refuse to be consigned to agriculture as in the past. Manufacturing offers advantages over agriculture, e.g., its flexibility in methods of competition and output; the fact that decreasing returns can be offset or postponed with rationalization or better organization; the ability of the industrialist to control the production process to meet demand and the ease with which a large number of workers can be managed. For these reasons, blacks are frequently drawn to industry even with limited capital.

In summary, entry into industry has been limited by lack of capital, education, and the presence of racial discrimination. Despite this, industrialization remains an attractive proposition to many who would escape from the demeaning, monotonous life of the agricultural laborer. Early enough some blacks engaged in nonagricultural occupations and became efficient artisans and mechanics. Some made headway in service industries, but as they grew in the North more people emigrated to that region for wage employment. Lack of requisite skills was an immediate handicap, and so was competition from poor whites. Good times came in war periods, just as depression and similar episodes witnessed unemployment for many.

Blacks had great success in industry due mostly to black fraternal and religious societies and to the state-owned Freedmen's Bureau. Among the successful areas were banking and insurance. There was noticeable achievement in other fields as well. In the 1960s and 1970s we observe a large degree of enthusiasm in black business with the trend toward Black Nationalism and Black Capitalism. The latter envisages black support of black communities and black businesses. Although there has been a growing participation of blacks in the American industrial sector and several government measures have been initiated to encourage the development of black entrepreneurs and executives, these projects were often doomed from the beginning. Black participation in the capitalist system could never result in the abundant life for most blacks.

6

The Black in the Labor Market

The labor market offers opportunities for the use of one's abilities and to the earning of an income for the procurement of life's necessities. The nature of the labor market, however, dictates whether these aims can be satisfied or not. Where it is free, resources should be efficiently allocated. Seekers of labor readily find the resources necessary to aid production. In the same way labor itself is able to seek rewards where it considers it most appropriate.

There are, nevertheless, certain imperfections in any labor market. Monopolies and monopoly practices, discrimination that can be economic and racial, ignorance of existing facilities due to lack of information, and poor transportation, to name a few, are the impediments to the free operation of the labor market. In a controlled regime, the state machinery controls the allocation of resources. Even here, ignorance and lethargy can clog the attempt and lead to wastages in material and human resources.

Our aim in this essay is fourfold. First, we shall examine in detail the nature and development of the living standards of blacks, which will relate to population, labor-force participation, nature of employment, and standard of living. Second, we shall explore the special case of black women and the variety of their activities in the different sectors of the economy. Third, we shall examine the occupational experience of black professionals, the aim here being to discover their experience in climbing the economic ladder. Finally, the aim is to study the influence of labor unions on black employment. With these as background, we should be able to make a reasoned forecast of the likely future of blacks in the American labor market.[1]

The disproportionate growth in the various sectors of the American economy has consequences that are disastrous for the low-income classes, among whom are the majority of blacks. This situation became evident with the catastrophe of the Great Depression of 1929-33 and the riots of 1965-69. These were grave reminders of the danger of the continuing inequality within the economy. The inequality is not static. It has been changing so that although blacks today may have a higher standard of living than in 1930, the gap between blacks and whites has remained the same or in most cases widened.

America is the principal capitalist nation. It has seven percent of the world's population and forty-two percent of its income. It has the highest per capita income and the highest nutritional standards for the average person. Per capita, United States citizens possess a greater quantity of goods that symbolize wealth and abundance: automobiles, telephones, radios, vacuum cleaners, electric lights, bathtubs, supermarkets, movie theaters, and hospitals. The nation's social ethics places emphasis on human ingenuity, initiative, adaptability, and enterprise. These qualities have enabled American citizens to expand the limits of production.

A system of equality is therefore feasible in the American society with its abundance of resources, so long as institutional and similar factors do not militate against it. Otherwise, personal economic inadequacy will be the result. This is the twofold tragedy of American affluence: the creation of waste in the economic situation and the fact that the abundance is practically unavailable to people of low-income levels, for they do not have the purchasing power to acquire it. Therefore, in an economy of abundance, the standard of living is raised, but is not attained by everyone, especially those living in economically and socially underpriviledged areas of the country. The per capita wealth of the nation is on an upward rise, leaving certain members of society with no noticeable surge, and even some with a downward trend.

If the minority class is to be economically improved, there must be a general awareness of what conditions exist and how these affect productivity. In the following pages we shall examine the economic conditions faced by many blacks in America. To be considered are population growth, labor force, employment, and standard of living.

POPULATION GROWTH AND CHARACTERISTICS

Although the majority of blacks have traditionally lived in the southern states, there is a noticeable trend away from the South within the past twenty years. In 1940 over three-quarters of all Afro-Americans lived in the southern states; practically all of the remainder lived in either the Northeast or the north central states. Ten years later the proportion of blacks living in the South had fallen to two-thirds. By 1960, three-fifths of the blacks resided in the South, and within six years that amount fell by five percent. In the early 1970s the trend away from the South stabilized, with some blacks even moving from the North back to the South.

While regionally the population has generally shown a noticeable trend away from the South and into the cities, the total black population, as a percentage of the total U.S. population, has remained relatively constant. As far back as 1900, blacks represented 12 percent of the total population; forty years later, that proportion had fallen only slightly to 10 percent. In 1960, blacks represented 11 percent of all Americans, and that figure stayed the same in 1966. What is interesting to note are the projections made by the government as to black population in the future. The most liberal estimate assumes that by 1980 blacks will be 13.5 percent and by 1990, 13.8 percent. Regardless of which projection is chosen, it appears that the black population will grow at a faster rate than the rest of the population.

One explanation for this faster growth may legitimately be

the youthfulness of the black population. The median age of the black male in 1968 was 38 percent lower than the median age of the white male. The black female median age was 33.5 percent lower than its white counterpart. There are about as many blacks less than five years old as there are blacks over fifty-five years of age. There are about one million more black females over age eighteen than black males over eighteen. In addition, from 1950, while the median age of the white population fell about 6.52 percent, the median age for blacks dropped about 19.2 percent. It may be more than coincidental that during this time span, not only did the black population grow noticeably younger, but black families also became more matriarchal. While the percentage of white families with both the husband and wife present remained about the same, from 1950 to 1966 that percentage for blacks fell from 77.7 percent to 72.7 percent. In 1950, 17.6 percent of all black families had a female head; by 1966, that percentage had risen to 23.7 percent.

Describing the population, however, is only a first step in our consideration of the economic problems facing black America. Of more relevance to the total picture is the black man's place in the labor force. Although blacks account for about 11 percent of the total population, they represent only 9.6 percent of the total labor force of 46 million. This may be explained in part by the youthful tendency we noted previously.

Within the expression labor force, as we mentioned, there are two branches—the employed and the unemployed. Perhaps no economic statistic, outside of the price indexes, has received as much public scrutiny recently as the unemployment figures. In recent years, most people have had reason to applaud these statistics. However, the black American has consistently had unemployment rates that approximated twice the national average. From 1964 until 1969, the American economy grew lustily, until by March, 1969, the unemployment rate fell to 3.5 percent. Yet during this entire time, the ratio of nonwhite unemployment to white unemployment was the same as it was during the economically more dismal 1950s. In 1955, nonwhite unemployment stood at a depressionlike 8.7 percent; for whites it was 3.9

percent; the resulting ratio was 2.2. In March, 1969, while only 3.1 percent of the white labor force was unemployed, black unemployment was 6.1 percent (much higher than the overall unemployment rate today when most economists are crying recession). Even though the economy had expanded greatly since 1955, the ratio of nonwhite to white unemployment still stood at 2.0. Clearly the economy has failed to accommodate Afro-Americans. In 1974 the rate of unemployment for blacks reached 15 percent.

TABLE 2
UNEMPLOYMENT RATE

	White	Non-White	Ratio: Non-White to White
1955	3.9	8.7	2.2
1956	3.6	8.3	2.3
1957	3.8	7.9	2.1
1958	6.1	12.6	2.1
1959	4.8	10.7	2.2
1960	4.9	10.2	2.1
1962	4.9	10.9	2.2
1964	4.6	9.6	2.1
1966	3.3	7.3	2.2
1968	3.2	6.7	2.1
1969, March	3.1	6.1	2.0

Source: 1955-1966 data from *Social and Economic Conditions of Negroes*, p. 30.
1968-1969 data from *Statistical Abstract*, p. 213.

Considering persons who are employed, we find even more evidence of the inability or unwillingness of the economy to meet black needs. First, besides considering unemployment, we must recognize the substantial underemployment that faces many blacks; underemployment is defined as either part-time workers seeking full-time employment or full-time workers earning less than $3,000 per year. From a study of low-income areas of nine large cities, the Labor Department has estimated that in these areas, underemployment is 2½ times greater than unemployment. Recognizing the heavy concentration of blacks in central city areas, we can imagine the staggering levels of combined under-employment and unemployment. Second, those blacks who are employed are, by and large, working in very low priority jobs.

In 1968, as in 1957, more workers were employed as blue-collar workers than any other occupational class. In 1957, 41.5 percent of all nonwhites worked in blue-collar jobs (over 85 percent of those were either operatives or nonfarm laborers). In 1968, 42.4 percent of all nonwhites worked as blue-collar employees (with operatives or nonfarm laborers accounting for 81 percent of that total). In both 1957 and 1968 service industries accounted for the second largest proportion of nonwhite employed; in 1957, service industries employed 32 percent of non-white labor force, in 1968, 28.3 percent. By 1968, white-collar workers surpassed farmworkers for third place in the nonwhite employment picture. Between 1957 and 1968, the percentage of nonwhites working in white-collar jobs almost doubled: from 12.8 percent in 1957 to 24.4 percent in 1968.

Half of that increase, though, was accounted for by a doub-ling, percentage-wise, in the number of clerical workers. Only in professional and technical jobs was there a respectable employ-ment increase. However, the percentage of nonwhites in these jobs is only slightly more than half the percentage of whites employed as professional or technical workers. We can receive a good impression of how miserable the economic system has failed by projecting the nonwhite employment situation in 1985. At this time all employed blacks will constitute 12 percent of the total labor force. Of these 7.8 percent will be in white-collar jobs, and 13.0 percent in blue-collar jobs, 23.7 percent will be service workers and 12.8 percent will be farm workers. If the present trend continues the level of nonwhites in prestigious jobs (white-collar jobs, craftsmen and foremen, and farm managers) will fail to reach full economic equality. In less important jobs, blacks will continue to fill a disproportionate share. Not only are blacks finding bad employment (when jobs are available), they will, in the future, without vigorous government assistance, continue to stay on the lower ranks of the employment ladder.

STANDARD OF LIVING

What is tragic, especially in view of the large number of young children, is that the poor employment situation is translated into poor income levels. Often, as we shall see, earnings are not related to the level of education one receives. In 1967, the median family income for all blacks was $4,919 or roughly 59 percent of the median white family income. Ten years earlier the nonwhite median income was 53.8 percent of the white level; in 1960, it had risen to 55.4 percent; in 1964, it had receded to 54 percent, only to rise in 1966 to 58 percent. One would certainly be justified in remarking at the progress made, but the fact remains that the median income for blacks is less than two-thirds that of his white counterpart.

Another way of looking at the income situation is to note that the distribution of income among blacks in 1967 approximates that of whites for 1955. The median income for nonwhite families in 1967 is less than the median income for white families in 1960, a recession year. The percentage of nonwhite families living below the established poverty level fell from 48 percent in 1961 to 35 percent five years later, as Table 3 illustrates. Although this index has shown a significant decline, when we relate this with the level of white poverty, the figures are not as impressive. In 1961, the proportion of nonwhite family poverty was 3.4 times as large as white family poverty; in 1966, that relationship was 3.5. Thus, while blacks are more and more escaping indigence, this tendency appears to be more an indication of the general economic picture, rather than a much needed boost from the economy for blacks.

Where this boost may come from may be shown by a correlation of the number of years one attends school to the median income. When this is done, one finds that a nonwhite who has

TABLE 3
PERCENTAGE OF FAMILIES
BELOW POVERTY LEVEL

	Non-White	White
1959	50	15
1960	49	15
1961	48	14
1962	47	13
1963	44	12
1964	39	12
1965	39	11
1966	35	10

Source: *Social and Economic Conditions of Negroes,* p. 22.

completed thirteen to fifteen years of school earns about as much as a white with nine to eleven years of school. This four-year lag is accentuated by the relationships between nonwhites with twelve years of school and whites with 8 years of school, or nonwhites with 9 to 11 years of education and whites with less than eight.

There is an obvious disparity in the level of living of whites and blacks. The education and income correlation confirms this inequality. The Great Depression of 1929 bore this out; political riots translated the economic insecurity of blacks into a sense of futility.

BLACK WOMEN IN THE LABOR FORCE

Black women have historically played an important part in the American labor force.[2] They have worked as domestic hands or on the farm. In 1890, 95 percent of the black working women were in the first category. In 1940, the number fell to 75 percent while 15 percent remained on the farm. In 1950 the figure for the domestic and farm hands dropped 53 percent. Those who left obtained white-collar jobs or were engaged as operatives in the service industries. But the change from private homes to commercial establishments did not necessarily mean an upgrade or real change in the nature of work. Some women found work in laundries, dry-cleaning, fabricated-textile manufacturing, and food processing.

Between 1910-1920 there was a decline in the black female labor force. A total of 1,997,207 black women were employed in 1910 whereas the figure was only 1,532,620 in 1920. Black men entered business and professions. Of the 52.8 percent blacks working in industries in 1910, 65.1 percent were males and 40.8 percent were females in 1920. Of the 46.1 percent blacks in industries, 62.4 percent were male and only 29.9 percent were female. The occupations most favored by black women were teaching, stenography, bookkeeping, secretaryship, textile work, waitressing, and hairdressing. The number of women employed in the doemstic services and farms declined considerably as more people sought education and moved to the North.

One explanation for the decline in the employment of black women since 1910 may be the sharp reduction in the employment of girls under twenty and women over sixty-five. The history of black women in America has been filled with heroics as well as the patient educating of children.

Harriet Tubman was a great abolitionist who, having escaped from her native city in Maryland to Philadelphia, devoted all her life to the migration of her fellow blacks to the North and East. As a leader of "freedom bands to Canada," she initiated the well-known "Underground Railroad" and became adept at smuggling people to freedom; she was called the "Moses of her race." During the Civil War, Harriet served as nurse, scout, and agent. She ranks with Frederick Douglass in the pantheon of black abolitionists. By her life and work, she demonstrated that women as well as men could contribute to the cause of human happiness.

In more modern times numerous women have distinguished themselves. Notable among them is Mrs. Carmel Carrington Marz, by profession an attorney. She was a legal advisor in the United States Mission to the United Nations in 1953. Privately she has served with various community groups. Edith Sampson on the other hand was an alternate delegate to the United

Nations 1950-53 under President Harry S. Truman and the first black woman to receive the Loyola Law Degree. A better-known figure in the music and diplomatic world was Marian Anderson, dscribed by J. Finley Wilson, himself a notable fraternal leader, as the "voice of a century." The U.S. government refused to allow her to sing at the Easter Sunday Celebrations of 1939 in Constitution Hall. In 1958-59 she was compensated by being appointed United States Alternate Delegate to the United Nations. Marian Anderson created much goodwill by subsequent tours to the Far East.

Black women also hold their own in the diplomatic field. An example is Mrs. Patricia R. Harris, former ambassador to Luxembourg, and the first woman to receive the J.D. from George Washington University Law School. Mrs. Harris has been active in both education and politics. In the area of civil service, we have such stalwarts as Jane M. Spaulding, Assistant to the Secretary, Department of Health, Education and Welfare, 1953-54. There is also Anna A. Hedgeman, Assistant to the Administrator, Federal Security Agency, 1949-53, and by profession a sociologist and educator. She is active in relief work and initiated educational programs for the Fair Employment Practices Commission under A. Philip Randolph in 1944.

Marie D. Gadsden has worked on the international front for the Peace Corps. Dr. Gadsden served as the English Program Director for the United States Information Service Program in Conakry, Guinea. Aileen Clark Hernandez was the only woman who served in the Equal Employment Opportunity Commission established by President Johnson under Title VII of the Civil Rights Acts of 1960. A graduate of Howard University, she developed keen interest in political science, became a trade unionist, teacher, researcher, writer, and civil rights fighter. In 1961 she was selected Woman of the Year by the Community Relations Conference of Southern California.

The 1970s produced numerous black women who captured the imagination of the public such as Angela Davis, Nikki Giovanni, and Frances Welsing.

THE OCCUPATIONAL EXPERIENCE
OF BLACK PROFESSIONALS

The opportunities for blacks to enter fields of occupation generally referred to as "professional" have been limited, and this accounts for the small number of those who are found in it. Black professionals, among whom are surgeons, dentists, lawyers, accountants, and clergymen, make up, according to a 1960 count, only 2.52 percent of the persons employed as professional or technical workers. This figure, when contrasted with the more than 10 percent that the black population comprises in the United States, shows how negligible is the class under discussion. In this section, our aim is to explore the extent, effect, and success of members of the black race in the professions as they seek to establish their own in the industrial structure of the nation.

There were virtually no black professionals existing before the Civil War. The institution of slavery in effect left little chance for such endeavors. Although isolated cases do exist, the number is so small as to be practically negligible.

After the war, however, black professionals made their first appearances in reasonably large numbers. Clergymen and teachers began to appear by 1866. These two professions claimed nearly all of the black college graduates until 1880. Black physicians and dentists began to practice in small numbers around 1870. Even fewer lawyers received degrees at that time. Social workers did not begin to come from the black race until around 1900. Perhaps the most revealing statistics concerning early black professionalism is that only ninety-six Blacks held professional degrees by 1876.[3]

Black professionals, besides being small in number, have faced the usual obstacles Blacks have faced in the United States since they were "freed." The white populace largely refused to patronize them and would not avail themselves of the skills of these black men. However, until very recently, white prejudice was not the only type of prejudice the black professional faced. Black people themselves, especially the middle class, have largely refused to be served by black professionals. Black doctors, for instance, would not seek black lawyers when they needed legal advice. The findings of A. B. Jackson, as reported in the 1933 *Journal of Negro History,* are very revealing in this regard:

> While in one of our large southern cities a few years ago a prominent Negro lawyer surprised me by saying that he did not employ a Negro physician. Pressed for a reason, he very frankly stated that it was because most physicians he knew did not stick to their profession enough to know medicine as they should, but delved into all sorts of other business for financial gain and practiced medicine almost as a sideline. They used their profession merely for the prestige it gave them in the community. Immediately I approached some of the physicians to find out about the lawyers, only to be told that when they needed a real lawyer they took their cases to a white member of the bar. The various reasons set forth were incompetent training of the Negro lawyer, crooked dealing, selling out, and many other such practices which violated professional ethics. Studying the case still further, I found that both professions condemned the clergy as a whole for numerous unprofessional acts, preying upon the ignorance of the poor people, preaching one gospel and practicing another. On the other hand, I found the ministers a bit more tolerant with the lawyers and the doctors than either group was toward them; but, if urged, they did not hesitate to cite various evidences of unprofessional conduct committed by their critics and admitted certain misgivings when they had to employ them.
>
> Since that time I have made a rather casual study of this unfortunate situation throughout the entire country and find that in too great measure this lack of confidence in the professional excellency of each other is generally prevalent.[4]

There is no doubt that this situation has seriously diminished opportunities for blacks in the professional occupations.

Up till this point, we have dealt with the professions generally. It will prove beneficial to deal with certain occupations separately. Consideration of professional occupations will therefore be divided into four categories for our discussion: physicians and dentists, lawyers, engineers, and others, the latter including teachers, social workers, and members of the clergy.

Blacks do not comprise a very large percentage of those persons employed in the medical profession. Only 1.97 percent of all doctors and surgeons are black; they total a little over four thousand in the United States. A slightly higher percentage of dentists, 2.146 percent, are black. This in total numbers represents approximately two thousand blacks. Moreover, the rate of increase for black doctors has been very slow during the last half-century. In 1900, there were 1,734 black physicians. This number was almost doubled by 1910 to 3,409 physicians. But since that time growth in number has been extremely slow for black physicians.

As previosuly mentioned, few black members of the medical profession existed before the 1860s. However, there were a few notable exceptions. The first known black doctor was James Derham, who acquired his medical knowledge under three separate masters, all of them doctors. His third owner gave him his freedom, and he built up an excellent practice by 1800.[5] Another notable black was Dr. James McCune Smith. A free Negro in New York City he studied abroad and entered the practice of medicine in 1837.

Education provides an interesting insight into the black and the medical profession. The typical black doctor was raised in a middle-class, literate home where the father was a man who was working at a job below his capacity because his color barred him from a better job. This suggests one reason why the number of black medical professionals is so low. Historically, the literacy level of blacks in the United States has been low, handicapping those interested in or capable of entering the medical profession.

Early in this century the black aspirants to the medical professions attended schools found mainly in the South. For undergraduate work, such schools as Howard University, Lincoln University, Morehouse College, and Fisk University were the choices of over seventy percent of all black preprofessionals. The Howard University Medical School along with several others in major southern cities accommodated the bulk of these students for their graduate work. Northern medical schools began applying strict quotas on Negro entrants after World War I, which decreased the already small number of Negroes obtaining medical education outside the South.

After 1947 this changed, and blacks began to attend predominantly white schools outside the South. However, most black medical students still attend predominantly black institutions.

Perhaps the most appalling situation presently is that although the percentage of blacks in the medical profession is small, it inexplicably fell even further about a decade ago and has probably continued to fall recently. Reasons for this situation are hard to pinpoint, and a complete answer is difficult, if not impossible, to find.

The legal profession is the nonscience occupation which has the smallest percentage of blacks as working members. Less than one percent of all lawyers are black. This may appear strange, because of the large number of blacks who have been deprived of their rights and who have required the services of an attorney. It would appear that given this circumstance, large numbers of blacks would find the legal profession inviting. However, circumstances have kept them from emerging in great numbers in the legal profession.

One reason for this is that historically the largest percentage of black persons in the United States have lived in the South. With the legal system operating as it has been in that region of the United States, blacks needing lawyers have been far better off to seek the counsel of white attorneys. Clients retaining black attorneys simply could not receive justice in the South. The only way a black defendant would have a reasonable chance of receiving a fair trial would be to appear in the courtroom with a "respectable white person."[6] Furthermore, disfranchisement of blacks, which occurred during Reconstruction, extinguished any chances a black lawyer might have in the South.

The North furnished isolated examples of successful black lawyers. Edward H. Morris was highly successful as counsel for both whites and blacks in Chicago, and William H. Lewis, a Harvard Law School graduate, had a distinguished law career in Massachusetts.

The migration of the black man to the cities in the North has aided the black lawyer. With greater chance to receive impartial treatment in the courts of the North, and the increasing black population of its cities, black attorneys have more opportunity to practice law and defend clients. As with the medical profession, most of the black lawyers come from families in which the parents were literate. Black lawyers are much more likely to have fathers who were white-collar workers than are nonprofessional blacks.

Black lawyers have received their education either at southern black schools or at predominantly white schools in the North. Howard University established a law school in 1871. Lincoln University in Pennsylvania had a law school, but for a short time only. Shaw University in Raleigh, North Carolina, and Straight University at New Orleans, Louisiana, both provided legal education for blacks by establishing law schools. The lack of black lawyers has led to a shortage of black politicians, for the legal profession offers more opportunities for entry into the field of politics than does any other profession. The inability of blacks to enter the legal profession has therefore effectively cut down on their chances to receive a greater voice in government.

In engineering, blacks have the worst record of employment. About one out of every two hundred engineers is black. The figures in each field—Aeronautical, Civil, Electrical, and Mechanical—show less than one percent of its total number to be black. The main reason for the small number of black persons in engineering is that the field is relatively new for blacks. Until recently, the only black institution where blacks have been able to receive such education is the School of Engineering at Howard University, which did not open until 1910. Since that date, only about one thousand persons have graduated in all fields of engineering combined. Graduates in electrical engineering lead the field with nearly four hundred graduates since the engineering school opened.

Of late, other predominantly black schools have established schools of engineering. North Carolina Agricultural and Technical College, Tennessee State Agricultural and Mechanical University, Tuskegee Institute in Alabama, and Prairie View

A & M College in Texas have each recently added engineering to their courses of study for students.

Blacks have the greatest professional representation in the fields of teaching, the ministry, social welfare, and recreation. In these professions, the percentage of the occupations that they comprise is close to the ten percent figure that blacks hold in the population generally. In the case of women, their representation in the field of social welfare and recreation exceeds this ten percent figure.

There are, perhaps, two reasons (which are interrelated) why representation in these fields is so much higher than in other fields. Because smaller salaries are paid in these occupations, less than in, for instance, the medical profession, perhaps there has been less desire on the part of the white man to keep the blacks out of these jobs. Also, to a certain extent, there is little competition between whites and blacks in these professions. For the most part, blacks have served blacks and whites have served whites, in these fields.[7] For instance, since whites excluded blacks from their churches, there was a definite need for black clergy members. Of course, laws in the South prohibited white teachers to teach black children, so black teachers were necessary there also.

These figures on teachers, clergymen, and social workers indicate that where the opportunity is unquestionably present, the black has entered the professions in fairly representative numbers. Seven percent of all teachers are black, while blacks make up ten percent of all social workers. In the field of religion, seven percent of all clergymen are black.

It is evident, therefore, that the educated, ambitious black has entered the professional fields in which obstacles were not too great, while most have either shunned the extremely difficult path of the other professions or fallen short of their goals.

The overall record of blacks in professional occupations is rather dismal. The circumstances prevailing in this country apparently have not been conducive to the development of the black professional. Factors contributing to this include white prejudice toward blacks, black mistrust of black professionals, and the lack of educational opportunities for blacks. Education appears to be the key; the fact that literate black families produce almost all black professionals and that middle-class black families produce a larger number than would be statistically normal indicate the extremely strong correlation between educational opportunity and the attainment of professional occupations.

The institutions to produce black professionals have been historically lacking, but recently the opportunities have begun to present themselves, both in the development of professional training at predominantly black institutions and in basically white institutions that have finally opened their doors to blacks.

Within the past few years, a major change has taken place in the policy of colleges and universities toward minorities and entrance patterns. This trend has manifested itself on most of the Claremont campuses, although questions concerning policies of certain admission offices have recently arisen. Far larger numbers of black students are being admitted to institutions of higher learning. The conclusion to be drawn from these facts is inescapable: the future will show an increase in black aspirants to professional occupations.

LABOR UNIONS AND BLACK EMPLOYMENT[8]

Workers band themselves into unions for a variety of reasons, chief of which is to protect their existing jobs, to prevent all forms of discriminatory practices, to achieve social security in jobs, and to obtain pension rights after retirement. While it was always legal for whites to form workers' associations, the law has frowned and in fact discouraged any such movement by blacks. Craft unions were the first to discriminate against blacks, and this continued for centuries till the birth of industrial unions, and yet there are still some unions that exclude blacks from becoming members. International unions have the best record so far in broadening the area of their membership. These unions set their face against racial discrimination, but their legislations or requirements are negatived by the local unions who carry out the dictates of the international unions.

The factors conditioning the discriminatory practices of the employment are first the prevailing image of the black worker as being ignorant and incompetent, which accusations died hard and continued to gain currency after they had been proved basically wrong. Then comes the general animosity of whites against blacks as competitors at jobs, or as elements used to thwart their own interests. For example, black workers were used to combat strikes, an action which brought down the ire of white strikers. As a result, pressure was brought to bar blacks in several places of employment from taking on jobs involving public contact. Where this was the case, unions and employers acquiesced in order at least to respect local feelings.

Not all the trade unions of today began as workers' associations as such. Some began as fraternal organizations whose membership was always restricted and which tended to take on racial overtones, catering for racial interests and aspirations. The railroad brotherhoods, for example, were among the first to begin in this way. For long they refused to include blacks, as this would mean the acceptance of racial equality. To the bogey of racism belonged also the fact of competition, especially so in the urban areas with their relatively large influx of black migrant workers. Here the whites who feared their job prospects threatened were the most opposed to black recruitment. They argued that black admission would depress wage levels, that the blacks did not possess relevant skills, and that there was the danger that blacks without the necessary qualifications might agitate for promotions based on seniority at jobs.

These open forms of discrimination have been fought right and left by the law courts, by Congress, and by private organizations like the NAACP. The many complaints filed against labor unions for their alleged discriminatory practices under the 1964 Civil Rights Act show to what extent formal exclusion in union membership and apprenticeship programs still persists, more particularly in the older unions than the industrial unions where organization on an industry-wide basis requires expansion in all the facets of labor within the particular industry, irrespective of the nature of employment. By way of illustration, the CIO, which is a predominantly industrial union, had fewer exclusion problems than the AFL, prior to the merger.

And now to the informal methods of discrimination these have many forms. Blacks and whites were hardly found in the same unions before 1930 and in the same way never shared jobs equally. Union constitutions spelled out the conditions of entry and these included racial discrimination. As community values changed and political and federation pressures increased, the local unions adopted other techniques like nepotism, segregated recruiting techniques, unfair examinations, the organization of black auxiliary unions like the Brotherhood of Railway Clerks and the sheet metal workers where the blacks were controlled by the white "parent" local. In such situations the rights of the black workers were seriously abused and their activities unnecessarily restricted.

In addition, the blacks were given little or no positions of leadership within the labor organizations that were expected to cater to their interest. This is typically the case of the International Ladies' Garment Workers, with its provisions preventing blacks from running for local and national offices. Nor were blacks consulted in such matters as strikes. The 1919 strike of the Railway Car Men was entered into without consulting the black workers. Other discriminatory techniques included unfair union hiring halls and referral systems, which effectively kept the blacks concentrated in menial jobs. Practices such as these were protected by contract agreements to the detriment of the black workers. Locomotive firemen, for example, entered into agreements, early in the century, to substantially reduce the number of black firemen, and as a consequence they restrained the opportunities of the blacks from reaching trainmen's status. Rigid examination tests were applied to blacks who desired promotion. It was in this way that the railroad unions limited opportunities for blacks.

A more dangerous method of union discrimination involved

the use of seniority rosters. This was disadvantageous to blacks in times of depression, when the rule "last come first fired" applied. Similar to this was the departmental roster, which was equally segregated. It meant that blacks could not move from one department to another, not even with promotions. This practice was nothing new. It has existed prior to the unionization movement but has been strengthened in later times. A typical example where separate seniority rosters were used was the oil industry.

The shipbuilding industry during World War I evinced the race-wage differential, whereby blacks received lower wages than their white counterparts. The same was true of the railroad locals, where black porters received less pay than their white colleagues, even though the former were assigned greater tasks than the latter.

The educational handicap of black workers was a part of the slave and plantation system. Artificial barriers were placed in their way of their acquiring any degree of literacy, and when this was being overcome employers and unions introduced the apprenticeship system, which limited the number of black entrants drastically.

The University of Texas Office of Manpower Policy, Evaluation and Research of the U.S. Labor Department, confirmed an old practice:

> Between March 1963 and March 1966 the Elevator Constructors Union in New York City admitted only two nonwhites to its apprenticeship training program. Local 2, Plumbers Union (Manhattan) admitted only nine. It admitted no nonwhite apprentices at all during 1965-66. . . . Sheet Metal Workers Local 28 admitted no nonwhites until 1966.

In the last instance it took a court order to force the union to open the apprenticeship program for blacks. Even after blacks were allowed to be tested for the program (and out of the top ten, nine were black), this union refused them entrance to the apprenticeship program, claiming that they had cheated.

In the building trades, several sheet metal workers locals

have always discriminated against blacks. Such was the case with the boilermakers and shipbuilders unions. It was thus difficult for blacks to benefit by the apprentice programs. Then came segregation on the plant level. Workers were segregated in their work places up to 1950. This was most conspicuous in industries with the largest concentration of blacks in the production area, for example, the tobacco industry, where the concentration was in the stemmeries, and in the Tobacco Workers International Union, where the segregated pattern obtains. The steel industry unions have clauses in their collective bargaining agreements to the disadvantage of the blacks with regard to wages, layoffs, and promotions.

The Brotherhood of Railway and Steamship Clerks had traditionally operated segregated locals in many northern as well as southern cities. In addition union agreements provided for separate racial classification, which limited black job mobility and violated the seniority of black members.

Management practices have also contributed their share to these discriminatory practices. It must be conceded that higher industrial education for blacks is a recent thing. In fact there was very little preparation for them prior to 1900. Business education lagged behind the classical and the theological. Black colleges following the established pattern gave little emphasis to business studies. A business education conference of 1899, held in Atlanta University, came out in full support for a change of emphasis on educational goals. It recommended that black colleges should prepare their students broadly and thoroughly for entrance into business activities and that the blacks themselves should participate more in business. Yet in 1924, there were only six black colleges offering business courses leading to a degree. In 1940 the number rose to twenty. The training emphasized specialization in banking, finance, insurance, transportation, marketing, foreign trade, statistics, economic history, labor, and economic theory. It is therefore not surprising that it is in banking, insurance, and finance that the black college graduates have made an appreciable breakthrough.

In spite of this rosy picture discrimination obtains still among the graduate employees. Few receive equal pay with their white colleagues, and fewer still rise above the management level. There is a heavy concentration in the lower medium of the industry salary scale.[9]

Owing to the discriminatory practices of many employers blacks still earn less than whites with the same level of education. The median income of a nonwhite male college graduate in 1960 was $5,020—actually $110 less than the earnings of white males with only one to three years of high school. A white man with four years of high school education can expect to earn about $253,000 in his lifetime. A black man with five years or more of college can expect $246,000 in his lifetime.

Furthermore, there are extremely few blacks occupying positions of responsibility in big business, like the large corporations, consulting firms, and the stock exchange houses. Oftentimes those who manage to be employed are used for window dressing or to do advertising and public relations jobs, especially to their race. Things are beginning to change, however, for under the pressure of the sit-ins, demonstrations and civil rights movements, and legislation, as well as the demand by black students and unions for relevancy, employment agencies are modifying their age-old tactics in favor of the blacks. Inside the unions themselves changes are taking place. Efforts are being made to eliminate discriminatory practices that stand in the way of black employment. The extent to which these efforts have succeeded will now be spotlighted.

The AFL founders were anxious from its inception to enforce the federation's equalitarian policies. It was in this light that they refused to admit the Brotherhood of Locomotive Firemen and the International Machinists Union, who had formal race bars in their constitutions. The AFL policy towards these two unions was however of little application to them, since the locomotive firemen continued to discriminate for many years after, and the machinists were later admitted after they had merely transferred their exclusion practices to union ritual. Denial of admission and moral persuasion were therefore ineffective devices in the light of the nineteenth-century racial attitudes. As a consequence, the federation officials adopted a "dual unionism" plan, having recognized the futility of their efforts. Under the plan, black locals were directly affiliated with the AFL when existing locals would not admit blacks. Many segregated locals were admitted after 1910, in the hope of compelling these unions to alter their practices. But this arrangement proved inadequate for the blacks.

The AFL has, since 1939, not admittd unions with formal race bars, but up till 1967, neither the AFL nor the AFL-CIO has expelled a union for exclusion practices. There have been instances in which individual unions have been instrumental in their efforts to eliminate union exclusion. The United Auto Workers once expelled a local for such practices. The Transport Workers and the American Federation of Teachers have pressured their locals to eliminate discriminatory practices.

Blacks, by the 1900s, realized the weight of discrimination and began their own trade unions. Because of the attitudes and practices of the constituent craft unions, leadership refused to insist upon integration of blacks into the unions themselves.[10] Consequently, blacks with skills such as longshoremen, hod carriers, and waiters organized their own unions. A black ship caulker, Isaac Myers, held union meetings called the Colored National Labor Convention as early as 1869.

The relationship between blacks and labor unions aroused interest in Dr. W. E. B. Du Bois. As a result he undertook a university study of black membership in unions in 1902 and reported that forty-three internationals including the railroad brotherhoods were without any black members and the twenty-seven additional unions had only a very small number of blacks.

Insofar as apprenticeship programs that unions sponsor were concerned, there has been a considerable lack of blacks involved. Yet most of the positive efforts have come in areas of economic expansion, times of public criticism, and cases where federal contracts, collective bargaining rights, and closed shops were at stake. Furthermore, the more constructive actions have been taken more for strategic reasons than for strong moral commitments. When blacks appeared to represent a potential force, they were joined by white workers, as in the trowel trades (bricklayers and plasterers in the South). Foremost in obliterating racial policies in trade unionism were the United Packinghouse Workers. It has all along supported black membership. Through such an attitude favoring blacks, some unions which had hitherto practiced discrimination were adversely affected. This was the case recently of AFL-CIO unions in Mississippi and Alabama. In these, local affiliates withdrew from the federations for racial reasons. Nevertheless there have been increasing attempts to remove discriminatory practices. Twenty-seven unions had formal exclusion clauses in their constitutions in 1923. This came down to fourteen in 1940, almost disappearing completely today.

The benefits of a strong labor movement cannot be gainsaid. Through it, government antidiscrimination legislation has been supported, so that in 1952, for example, Thurgood Marshall of the NAACP could claim that "the program of the CIO has become a Bill of Rights for Negro labor in America." As recently as 1964, the AFL president, Mr. George Meany, played a significant part in the insertion of the equal employment sections of the 1964 Civil Rights Act. This does not mean that all is well with the unions, since the mere insertion of the nondiscrimination clause does not mean total acceptance or even implementation. The local union leaders are still active and uncooperative in their opposition to black admission.

7 | Black Entrepreneurship

The tendency to think of the entrepreneur in the popular but restricted sense of innovator or organizer obscures the functions and blurs an understanding of this important person in the development process. There is no yardstick for categorizing entrepreneurial functions. Size or cost alone of inventions is not a sufficient measure. Neither is the impact of the activity a sufficient index of the entrepreneurial function.

The entrepreneur possesses creativity, the ability to evolve new ideas and to adapt existing resources efficiently to changing situations and processes. Where such people exist, and there are conditions favorable to their use, economic development moves at a faster pace. Either out of necessity, luck, chance, or design the entrepreneur dreams. His motives may be spiritual ambition, snobbery, love or power, joy of creating, the desire to excel, or to prove the quality or superiority of his race. We can distinguish three main categories of entrepreneurs:[1]

1. Those whose ideas changed the course of life of others.

2. Those whose inventions changed economic life.

3. Those who organize and manage enterprises, the coordinators of factors of production.

82

THE SOCIO-ECONOMIC IDEAS
OF SOME BLACK LEADERS[2]

Individuals whose ideas, thoughts, and suggestions alter the course of events are as good entrepreneurs as the men who execute. They may not perform the overall coordinating function of bringing together the factors of production, but they could be innovators and men of ideas. These ideas do not have to be appealing to be important. As J. M. Keynes rightly said:

> The ideas of economists and political philosophers, both when they are right and when they are wrong, are more powerful than is commonly understood. Indeed, the world is ruled by little else.

Of those whose ideas changed economic life, we include W. E. B. Du Bois, Booker T. Washington, and Malcolm X. To them belonged the capacity to dream, to move out of the beaten track, to see new opportunities and be confident of success in the face of objective obstacles. The ideas and programs of such men merit a scientific, objective, and impartial scrutiny and presentation. Their impact on the economic lives of blacks warrants attention from all.

W. E. B. Du Bois[3]

Du Bois' ideas on self-help, "group economy," socialism, and international economic cooperation were developed as the vehicle for the economic emancipation of the black race. To Du Bois, self-help was of prime importance to advancement. As a consequence he favored increased contact between races since the lack of it would generate suspicion and foster economic discrimination, which in the end would harm blacks more than the whites. Blacks had the duty to elevate themselves by the establishment of enterprises for the provision of employment, training in skills and the rendering of useful services. College education would prepare a person for this, giving broad insight into the business world and producing "captains of industry." Further, by pooling small savings, cooperating in business, and patronizing their own goods and establishments, blacks could regain their lost heritage as a race. A penny bank, Du Bois stressed, was more useful than the vote. Both, however, were necessary and significant.

Through *Horizon,* the unofficial organ of the Niagara Movement, Du Bois pushed his theory of "group economy." He insisted that blacks support and control their own institutions with their own ideas leading to their own identity. Du Bois demanded political, industrial, and social equality through the pages of the *Crisis,* the unofficial organ of the NAACP. His idea of equality was not to be equated with sameness, but was rather the "right of diversity," the right to opportunities commensurate with the individual's capacities and needs. To illustrate this equality Du Bois argued for industrial freedom so that the black man would have a voice in the conditions of his labor.

Du Bois' economic cooperation was that of wealth accumulation for collective rather than industrial welfare. It was not enough to own homes, land, and other forms of physical capital, but the people should also form cooperation at the various stages of production, distribution, and exchange. With the gains from these they could apply them to practical ends like social welfare and the tackling of political issues.

His type of socialism, which became the dominant philosophy of his life from the Niagara Movement Foundation, was not committed to any particular path of right or left wing sect. This "Socialism of the Path" according to him meant a limited ownership of the public wealth by the state and not necessarily the complete abolition of private property. This form of socialism would, he believed, save blacks from the oppressions of the capitalist, the "idle rich." It would also temper the greed and corruption in society.

His advocacy of self-help, group economy, and, at the same time, a certain amount of racial intercourse was due to what he called the "puzzling dilemma" of blacks, Americanity, and Africanity. Du Bois, to reconcile this, suggested a cultural pluralism that gave due accent to the mission of the black race and its contribution to American society and the maintenance of a reasonable living standard, if possible, by separate racial, educational, and business institutions. To achieve the last objective, the worker, he insisted, should have the franchise, for without the vote, he could not retrieve his grievances nor ameliorate the harsh economic conditions that beset him.

Du Bois was also a pioneer in African economic independence. He was one of the first Americans to identify himself with Africa and to stress the strong connections which the blacks in America had with the home of their ancestors. He showed the many links between the two, the strong influence of the family, the supporting programs and activities of mutual aid societies and the proverbial skill of the black artisan dating back to the achievements made in ancient Egypt in North Africa and Benin in West Africa. Du Bois was at one time secretary of a company interested in East African economic advancement. In the Pan-African congresses which he sponsored from 1919-1945, Du Bois reiterated at an international level his philosophy of black solidarity, the right of Africans to their land and to its proceeds, the proper regulation of labor, and the spread of technical and liberal education for all blacks in Africa as well as in America. He, nevertheless, favored unionization of all races working in an industry, just as he welcomed the fullest participation of all races as partners and not as exploiters and the exploited in the world economy.

Booker T. Washington[4]

Booker T. Washington lived between the nineteenth and the twentieth centuries in America, in the age of "market princes" and "robber barons," an era when men of humble beginnings created large financial empires. Washington's age emphasized the productive capacity of men, and derided the slothful and ne'er-do-wells.

Socially the era witnessed an advocacy of the racial inferiority of blacks and the superiority of whites in every field of human endeavor. While the industrial revolution brought wealth to many whites, it presented great obstacles to blacks who were beginning for the first time to experience freedom from slavery.

Washington, cognizant of the racial and economic situation, advocated a philosophy of self-help, industry, and wealth suitable to the black condition and capable of enabling them to earn their rights as citizens of the United States in the future. His type of industrial and technical education, deprecated by some radicals as retrogressive, was to be the preparatory ground for the professions. "I plead for industrial education and development for the Negro not because I want to cramp him, but because I want to free him. I want to see him enter the all-powerful business and commercial world."

The black person, he believed, must work his way up, at whatever job he may possess. By gradually improving his economic situation and by developing habits of thrift and industry he would qualify for the respect of whites and therefore for civil liberties. Not to antagonize the poor whites who also needed to be employed in the new industries in the South and to ease the way for the acceptance of blacks not long ago emancipated from slavery, Washington advocated the cultivation of bourgeois virtues but also the development of wealth and property ownership among blacks.

Washington stressed that success came to him who had been courageous to overcome great difficulties, that the more the risk the greater the gain. He believed also in the doctrine of free competition and rugged individualism and in the power that the possession of wealth confers on its owner. Wealth to him was the panacea of the ills of blacks and the energies of the race were to be devoted to its achievement.

Washington's economic philosophy was drawn from the facts of life. His earlier acquaintance with Hampton Institute had convinced him of a few facts of life, which were later to find fruition in his speeches and work. These facts of life could be summed up in the words: accommodation, industry, and racial solidarity. What influence had Hampton Institute on him? This is seen in the philosophy of General Samuel Armstrong, the founder, that labor was a "spiritual force, that physical work not only increased wage-earning capacity but promoted fidelity, accuracy, honesty, persistence, and intelligence." In his Tuskegee

Experiment, Washington became the exponent of these ideas and maintained that the best way for his people to participate in the American economy was through industrial education.

The advocacy of this view was nothing revolutionary or novel because the slavery period was the foundation for black artisanry. Paul Lawrence Dunbar maintained in August, 1898, that the black had already proved his manual efficiency in the plantations as blacksmith, carpenter, and shoemaker.

Washington's work here was memorable because he pioneered a school for blacks in which he proved the usefulness and applicability of his theory. The helpless condition of blacks at the time made him disinclined to press for social equality. He therefore advocated a type of education that would prove blacks were not indolent and that would be beneficial to both races.

His students provided the white community services and products that they needed, and in these ways wore down their hostility. In this form of cooperative effort he can be considered as an entrepreneur. His system of industrial or vocational education meant the establishment of a satisfactory economic and social equilibrium between blacks and whites. This strategy was, of course, an attempt to conciliate the two races.

On black participation in business, Washington accepted as a point of departure the dominant competitive philosophy of American business. He believed that in a free market the forces of supply and demand will operate without regard to color; that success in business would ensue with industry and good-neighborliness. These are extensions of the classical political economic teachings of free competition and rugged individualism. Herein lies one weakness of his philosophy. The small capitalist, in spite of goodwill, stood little chance of success in the face of the rising octopus of the modern industrial and business machinery with its huge capitalization and complex organization. Washington showed little understanding of these realities. The same criticism can be extended to his view on management relations—his counseling workers to submit to their employers—since unionization would be regarded as creating a sort of enmity.

Though Washington's business philosophy was restricted his

practical execution of this was striking and heroic. He appealed to fellow blacks to enter business and manufacturing. The Fourth Atlanta University Conference held in 1898, which was sponsored largely by Booker T. Washington, called on blacks to enter into business life in increasing numbers, to patronize business enterprises conducted by their own race, even at some slight disadvantage. The conference called for the dissemination of information on the need for black business and the organization of local, state, and national Negro business men's leagues.

Booker T. Washington as a follow-up to this meeting called a national meeting of black businessmen in Boston in 1900. He was elected the first president of the National Negro Business League by the more than one hundred delegates from thirty-four states attending the conference. He pushed further his idea of black participation in business by the issue of his book *The Negro in Business*. In this book he enumerated the success stories of many businesses since the first year of the league's existence, which included grocery stores, restaurants, drug stores, merchandise stores, tailoring establishments, building, confectionaries, cooperative stores, banking, and insurance.

Washington believed in the liberation of blacks through their own efforts. Though he did not favor political or social equality, he made contributions to lawyers who challenged segregation laws. By his appeal to wealth, he was calling attention to the basic problem facing the black in the South, namely, capital deficiency. Most black farmers lacked the necessary capital for the purchase of land and the marketing of their products. Capital could only be lent at exorbitant interest rates. Agricultural depression, crop failures, and the evils of farm tenancy and sharecropping made profitable farming impossible for blacks.

Washington proposed two remedies for this problem: making farming productive by staying on the land instead of migrating to the North and better husbanding of the soil by rationalization. His plan was eventually to develop a substantial propertied class of landowners who would be their own employers. For this he appealed to the racial pride and solidarity of the black race and urged them to imitate the Jews who through unity and faith were becoming more and more successful. At the farmers' meetings in Tuskegee, Washington discussed the evils of the mortgage system, the one-room cabin, buying on credit, the importance of owning a home and of saving money in the bank.

Washington was one of the few black spokesmen with faith in the South. *The Man Farthest Down,* published in 1912, epitomized a life-long opinion that the economic future of blacks lay in the South and that in spite of apparent unwelcome experiences their lot was better than their counterparts elsewhere. By using his peculiar tactics he hoped to lift them out of their rut. His adroit manipulation of ambiguous statements made him more liked than feared. His influence with philanthropists and politicians was tremendous, and he used it to good advantage. Carnegie, Rosenwald, the Phelps-Stokes and Jeanes funds, and the General Education Board rallied round him and sought his advice on the qualifications of black schools for support. Theodore Roosevelt made him "adviser" on black affairs and political appointments and patronages were distributed not without his consultation.

If Washington was convinced that his were the methods for every black to rise he was laboring under a colossal delusion, because the odds were definitely against them. Looked at from another angle, this weakness of his was a source of encouragement for others. Entrepreneurs who fail can teach others success by their failures.

Washington's opposition to labor unions stemmed from his dislike for the clandestine activities of labor leaders who either defrauded the workers or fomented trouble for them. He observed that racial discrimination and antagonism increased the number of blacks used as strikebreakers. This would not happen, Washington believed, if black labor remained free and docile. To the agitators he counseled: "An inch of progress is worth more than a yard of complaining."

As a compromise for his extreme view on political agitation and participation, he proposed educational and property tests that would apply to both races and that would do away with corrupt and incompetent governments. Washington's ambiguity and realism are also seen in his secret campaigns against disfranchisements and discrimination, political lobbying, collection, and disbursement of money to fight electoral provisions and juridical structures inimical to blacks. Thus Washington excelled in behind-the-scenes activities, fanning racial solidarity without preaching racism, deprecating protest and agitation but supporting them when he thought it fit to do so. Washington, while advancing his physiocratic ideas on the value of the soil and the development of Negro yeomanry, did not fail to praise the captains of industry who supported black institutions.

Booker T. Washington's influence was far reaching. His advocacy of the philosophy of self-help, racial solidarity, and economic development was as enthusiastic as his plea for political and civil rights was moderate. He wielded a strong influence among state officials and southern businessmen and others who were dependent on southern markets and used this to the advantage of his friends and black educational institutions.

Malcolm X[5]

The inclusion of Malcolm X in this survey is based on the importance of his socio-economic ideas and the wide influence that these have had in the economic history of blacks in America. Malcolm X's ideas were a revulsion agaisnt a whole range of tenacious and pervasive myths about the black man in America and the unremitting influence of the news media on the entire culture. These myths include: the rural southern belief in the "childish nature" of the black man; the belief in the "natural sinfulness" of the urban black man found among the residents in southern and northern cities; and the more modern myth of the "moderate" politicians who claim that all the black man needs is an "equal opportunity" in employment, and that laws to do this only need be passed and all will be well.

Malcolm X, to combat the above myths and to bridge the gap between whites and blacks, advocated economic nationalism by which blacks would control their own communities. His words recall those of Du Bois and Garvey of four decades or so earlier for a group economy or a separate black nation. For example in a speech delivered at Harvard, Malcolm X said, inter alia:

> Our economic philosophy of Black Nationalism means that instead of our spending the rest of our lives begging the white man for a job, our people should be reeducated to the science of economics and the part that it plays in our community. We should be taught just the basic fundamentals; that whenever you take money out of the neighborhood and spend it in another neighborhood, the neighborhood in which you spend it gets richer and richer, and the neighborhood from which you take it gets poorer and poorer.
>
> This creates a ghetto, as now exists in every so-called Negro community in this country. If the Negro isn't spending his money downtown with what we call "the man," "the man" is himself right in the Negro community. All the stores are run by the white man, who takes the money out of the community as soon as the sun sets. We have to teach our people the importance of where to spend their dollars and the importance of establishing and owning businesses. Thereby we can create employment for ourselves, instead of having to wait to boycott your stores and businesses to demand that you give us a job.

In his *Autobiography,* Malcolm X came out more forcefully in his advocacy of black control. He remarked:

> The Black man in America is economically sick and that is evident in one simple fact: as a consumer, he gets less than his share, and as a producer gives least. For instance, forty percent of the expensive imported Scotch whisky consumed in America goes down the throats of the status-sick Black man; but the only black-owned distilleries are in bathtubs, or in the woods somewhere. Or for instance—a scandalous shame—in New York City, with over a million Negroes, there aren't twenty black-owned businesses employing over ten people. It's because Black men don't control and own their own community's retail establishments that they can't stabilize their own community.

Taking the salient points in Malcolm X's writings we observe that in the first quotation he insisted that ghetto poverty is created by white businesses that syphon the little financial resources in the ghetto in the form of high prices and other monopolistic devices. His theory and solution are reminiscent of mercantilism with its advocacy of internal development with less intervention by those living outside the particular community. Like the mercantilists he strove for favorable balance of trade, by which the ghetto's business relationship with "outsiders" should always be in the former's favor.

The weakness of applying the mercantilist arguments must, of course, be underlined. It is not by the conservation and consumption of local resources that the standard of living of the people can improve. While this strategy is beneficial to business-men who want to dispose of their goods at all costs, it does not add to the welfare of the particular community economically. What is beneficial is the free movement of goods and services, that is, their accessibility at competitive prices. It would be sound economics to advocate for domestic consumption, since the industries will be producing for outside consumption; the self-sufficiency policy will generate a boom and consequently more employment. Granted the argument is more applicable to countries; yet, if the ghetto is treated as a "special disaster area," needing protective measures of all sorts, it is possible to attain these ends, and with the preference, expand income and production.

Malcolm X's tirades against blacks themselves make him more a Bookerite than a Garveyite. The black man in the ghettoes, he insisted, has to start self-correcting his own material, moral, and spiritual defects and evils. The black man needs to start his own program to get rid of antisocial behaviors. The black man in America has to lift up his own sense of values.

The real problem, according to Malcolm X, lies in poor education, demeaning types of jobs, the pathology of the ghetto, and a host of others associated with them. The way out, accord-ing to him, is not for a few "token Negroes" to be successful, while the majority are trapped in poverty. Rather, "the American black man should be focusing every effort on building his own businesses and decent homes for himself. As other ethnic groups have done, black people, wherever possible, should patronize their own kind, hire their own kind, and start in those ways to build up the black race's ability to do it for itself." Only in these ways, he said, will the American black ever get respect. For these and for the removal of all barriers to economic opportunities that give one group an advantage over another rather than for an autarchy.

Malcolm X's arguments have, however, at least two redeeming facts: the need for consumer economics and the possibilities of employments creation. Malcolm X rightly emphasized the need for economizing scarce resources in the ghetto. Despite his low income level, the average ghetto dweller spends a considerable part of his income on durables and oftentimes luxuries as well. Imitating the American image of acquiring material possessions as a sign of prestige and comfort, he depletes his own resources for more useful items. Color television sets, Cadillacs, and similar appliances are the vogue for those who find no other way of equaling the Joneses.

To complicate things further, the ghetto dweller is presented with a limited variety of goods from which to choose. He ends up buying things at a high price or sometimes of an inferior quality. Where he cannot pay on the spot, the ghetto businessman usually allows him "easy" installment payments, which eat into the future incomes of the buyer. It is to safeguard these occurrences that Malcolm X insisted on a separate development of the ghetto.

In what way has Malcolm X changed the self-image of blacks and in what way have whites been affected by his presence? He tried to free blacks mentally and spiritually from their crippling dependency on the white man's favors and moods. He completely opposed the ever-present influences in America that constantly try to persuade the black man in America that he is inferior from the moment he is born to the day he dies. The religious doctrine of the dominant society, he maintains, is oftentimes so different from what is preached that it undoes a lot of the previosuly instilled "yes-boss" training. The elimination of inferiority-complex can be at least indirectly traced to the rise in black cultural pride, for which Malcolm X deserves some credit. Black pride, if not black power, owes a great deal to Malcolm X.

What does white America owe Malcolm X? He taught it to respect the black man, all the time reminding it that the ghetto mentality, criminality, violence, and fatalism stem from what the society has done to keep it in slavery for centuries. To both races he left a clear picture of ghetto life with its problems and prospects.

BLACK INVENTORS AND INNOVATORS: THEIR ECONOMIC IMPACT

Inventors add a new dimension to economic life by introducing an element that maximizes existing resources.[6] The invention of the locomotive engine for example was the prelude to an increase in velocity, a decrease in cost, and a greater safety in the running of trains. Similarly, by the assemblage of information and its analyses, the innovator achieves a result of novel combinations of factors. Innovation is usually a controlled, directed, and purposeful human activity, aiming at producing changes that improve a system.

Blacks whose inventions revolutionized economic life are not hard to find. They include Norbert Rillieux, Elijah McCoy, Jan Earnest Matzeliger, and George Washington Carver, just to name a few. By their inventions they developed, chiefly for their masters, new processes or combinations of them to the satisfaction of certain economic ends. In the same way black innovators introduced new production methods and forms of organization important to social and economic development.

Why is it that our American public has long been ignorant of the contributions made in the field of invention and innovation by members of the black race? Several situations seem to contribute to this result. There has been a strong bias in American history and writings preventing them from attributing to blacks their rightful place for their additions to man's stock of knowledge and advancement. Early on, slaves could not receive patents for their inventions. This resulted in the failure of the public to recognize black inventors. Also, patent records, with one notable exception to be discussed later, failed to record the race of patent recipients. Finally, the general disinclination of most whites to recognize Negro achievements adds to the myth that the blacks have not made significant contributions in the fields of invention and innovation.

We shall now discuss briefly the achievements of blacks who have furthered the knowledge of technology and history through their inventions and innovations. In this connection we shall discuss the contributions of such inventors as Henry Blair, Elijah McCoy, Norbert Rillieux, Granville Woods, Garrett Morgan and Jan Matzeliger, and those of two innovators, Carter G. Woodson and John H. Johnson. Their roles to the field of black history and the projection of the black race are important and therefore deserving of careful study.

Henry Blair received what is believed to be the first patent issued to a black in 1834.[7] This was in recognition of his corn-planting device. Two years later he received his second patent, this time for a cotton-planting machine. Blair's case is interesting because it is the only instance in which the Patent Office registry recorded the race of the patent recipient. Blair was evidently a freedman, because slaves could not legally receive patents.

Elijah McCoy, a Canadian-born black who did most of his scientific work in Michigan, was perhaps the first person to develop the concept of aiding the lubrication process in machinery, an idea that has attained greater importance as machines have become more complex and more widely used. He developed methods for automatic lubrication. His single most important invention along these lines was probably the lubricating "drip Cup," a tiny container filled with oil that controlled the flow of oil to the essential moving parts of heavy-duty machinery by means of a "stopcock."[8] This device quickly came into general use on the leading railroads and ships around the world. This cup was the key device necessary for the perfecting of the overall lubrication system used in large industry today.

McCoy patented numerous other devices also. He received fifty-seven patents for inventions designed to streamline his automatic lubrication system.[9]

Norbert Rillieux, whose mother was a slave and whose father was a wealthy engineer, was born on the latter's plantation in 1806. He went to France to receive his higher education in Paris. His engineering and scientific skill won him an appointment as an instructor in applied mechanics at a special institution.

In 1845 he invented a new method of refining sugar that utilized a vacuum evaporating pan. This device consisted of condensing coils in vacuum chambers. This method radically revolutionized the sugar refining industry. Previously, sugar had been refined in a rather crude manner, utilizing gang slave labor. Large numbers of slaves would laboriously ladle boiling sugar-cane juice from one kettle to another. This process was known as "the Jamaican Train." Not only did Rillieux's invention do away with the need for this gang labor, but the product was vastly superior to that obtained by the old method, and it cost less for a company to produce.

The first Rillieux evaporator was installed at a plantation in Louisiana in 1845, and the innovation quickly spread to other United States areas and to other countries that produced a large amount of sugar, such as Mexico and Cuba.

Rillieux returned to Paris in 1854, and after his evaporator process was adopted in Europe he devised a way to apply this new process to the sugar beet. His method cut sugar beet production and refining costs in half. He made another important contribution to mankind, but this was unfortunately rejected due to prejudice. He developed a workable and practical method for a sewage system in New Orleans. The authorities of that city, however, refused to implement his plan, choosing not to accept the plans of a black man. Of course, the lack of an adequate sewage system was largely responsible for the epidemics of yellow fever that occurred regularly in that city. Avoidance of such epidemics probably would have been the result of the installation of Rillieux's system. However, New Orleans bigotry netted that city numerous unnecessary deaths at the hands of yellow fever.

A very prolific inventor and patent recipient was Granville Woods. His inventions were great in both quantity and diversity. He was born in Columbus, Ohio, in 1856, and, after a short formal education, began to work with mechanical devices. He worked in a machine shop for a time, then took a job with a railroad company and later with a rolling mill. He went to college to study mechanical engineering and became a railroad engineer.

Shortly thereafter, he began his inventing career. His first patent, for a steam boiler furnace, was obtained in 1884. His most important invention was probably his next major one, which he patented in 1887. It was a Synchronous Multiplex Railroad Telegraph, which was designed and used to avert railroad accidents by allowing trains and their personnel to be informed at all times about the whereabouts of the trains ahead and behind their particular position. It also served to warn engineers of problems on their routes.

He also invented an incubator, the forerunner of today's huge incubators, in 1900. He received three patents for electric air brakes, in 1902, 1903, and 1905.

Later, he invented fifteen appliances to aid in electrical control and distribution for railroads. He organized his own company, the Woods Electrical Company, early in his career. This company took over most of his early patents, but as he gained stature in the scientific world his inventions appreciated in value, and a ready market was available for many of these inventions. Some of the companies that bought rights to his inventions were the General Electric Company, the Westinghouse Air Brake Company, the American Bell Telephone Company, and the American Engineering Company.

Granville Woods and his brother, Lyates Woods, collaborated on the joint invention of several items. Two of the previosuly mentioned air brakes patents were recorded jointly, as was an invention for transmitting messages by electricity.[10]

It is the opinion of some historians that Woods had a creative genius covering a wider range than any other black inventor, and that his versatility ranks high among all inventors.

Garrett Morgan was another black inventor whose invention was not as readily accepted as it would have been had he not been black. This situation probably led to more problems for the persons exhibiting prejudice than it did for Morgan. He was born in Kentucky in 1877, but he soon moved to Cleveland, which remained his home for most of his life up until his death, which occurred in 1963.

His first invention was an improvement of the sewing machine, an idea he sold for 150 dollars. His major invention was the gas inhalator, which he developed shortly after his sewing machine improvement. Its value was demonstrated when a tunnel explosion trapped several men in the Cleveland Waterworks 200 feet below the surface of Lake Erie. With his brother and two volunteers, all wearing the gas inhalators, Morgan was able to descend into the tunnel, filled with gas and smoke, and save the victims from asphyxiation. This incident gave the gas inhalator a large degree of publicity, which resulted in numerous orders for the new mask. However, when Morgan's racial heritage became known, many of the orders were canceled. Morgan himself could not even demonstrate the inhalator in the South; he had to employ a white man to do so.

During World War I, Morgan's invention was transformed into a gas mask for United States combat troops. After the war, in 1923, Morgan was able to sell his invention of an automatic stop sign to the General Electric Company for forty thousand dollars, a fee his reputation as an inventor made possible.

Jan E. Matzeliger was a man who made only one major contribution to the field of invention. However, his invention assumes a great degree of importance when the results of this invention are discussed, and he therefore is usually considered to be the black who has made the most significant contribution to the field of invention. His contribution is often equated with those of Eli Whitney and Elias Howe.[11]

Matzeliger was born in Surinam in 1852 to a wealthy white engineer, in charge of the government machine works, and a native black woman. He first began to work with machines at the age of ten, when he went into apprenticeship in a shop run by his father. After showing considerable skill in the field of mechanics, he went to sea with an East Indian merchantman at the age of nineteen. After two years at sea, he entered the United States and settled in Philadelphia in 1874. After a short time working at odd jobs, including probably as a cobbler, he moved to Boston and then Lynn, Massachusetts, where he began work in a shoe factory in 1877. He held numerous odd jobs in addition to his factory job in the following few years.

While he was moving from town to town and from job to job, the shoe industry was looking for a way to last shoes. Machines had been developed to cut, tack, and sew shoes properly, but hand lasting was still the only method available to manufacturers. This primitive method worked in the following manner: after the worker hooked the last in a holding-jack, "He laid the innersole on the bottom of the last. Then placing the upper leather, that had been cut to conform, over the last, he drew into position the edges of the upper and tacked them fast to the innersole." This process was a slow and tedious one, requiring a skill which took several years of apprenticeship to develop.

In 1872, Gordon McKay organized the McKay Lasting Association in an attempt to find a workable lasting machine among the numerous patents. His company spent a quarter of a million dollars on devices and research, culminating in the production of a device known as the McKay Laster. McKay consolidated with another group with a similar machine to form the McKay and Copeland Lasting Association, putting the best features of each into one laster. However, the effort was a vain one. Although the machine could last heavy shoes and boots, it was virtually useless on regular styles.

While these efforts were occurring and failing, Matzeliger was working in a shoe factory in Lynn and attempting to invent a lasting machine in his small amount of spare time. In 1880, after six month's work, he finished his first machine, made out of scraps of wood, wire, and cigar boxes. Believing himself on the proper path, he set out to improve his invention. He was able to obtain a small area to work on his invention in a shoe factory where he had access to the necessary tools. He completed an iron version of his machine and began to search for financial backing. After a long effort, he found two wealthy citizens of Lynn who would support his venture for one-third interest each in the finished product. He obtained a patent for his machine in 1883, and in 1885 his machine successfully passed its first factory lasting test.

Immediately, numerous persons became interested in producing Matzeliger's product. The Union Lasting Machine Company bought the patent for a block of stock. Several other companies became involved with Matzeliger's invention. Eventually, Sydney W. Winslow bought the patent and formed the United Shoe Machinery Company, which absorbed over forty corporations. A capital stock of $20 million was soon built up and after 20 years this increased to $242 million. This invention also resulted in a 50 percent reduction in the price of shoes. It doubled wages and improved working conditions for millions of people working in the shoe industry.

Unfortunately, Matzeliger did not live to see his efforts result in such success, nor did he have a chance to receive the enormous financial benefits properly his. Due to the extreme hardship he had undergone before his invention, he was in poor health and died in 1889 at the age of thirty-seven.

George Washington Carver, the greatest of black inventors, was born in Missouri in 1864. His fame as an innovator lies beyond his Tuskegee laboratory and stretches into the corridors of American and world scientific research.[12] Born in the age of revolutionary methods in agriculture, George Washington Carver made his mark in Tuskegee where in 1896 he came to direct the department of agricultural research. It was there that he became an authority on soil and plant life.

Early on he worked on joint programs of the state with the Alabama Polytechnic Institute, on a monograph of the Tungi; the Division of Agrostology of the Department of Agriculture at Washington, on grass specie; and with the Smithsonian Institute, on medicinal flora of the country. These, no doubt, brought him much recognition, but it was more in his pioneering work among farmers—whom he advised and whose water, cattle, and flora he analyzed—that he is mostly remembered.

Carver was an authority on peanuts, and it is said that he devised over 300 ways of using the product. At the Ways and Means Committee of the United Peanut Association, which met in Montgomery in 1920, he discussed the various uses of peanuts. This gave the peanut industry a greater impetus by the increase in demand. The Fordney-McCumber Bill of the said Ways and Means Committee wrote the highest tariff rate the peanut industry ever had. The *Peanut World* described him as "that incomparable genius to whose tireless energies and inquisitive mind the South and the country owe so much in the development of the peanut trades, arts and industry." The practical result was a shift of Coffee County from cotton to peanut culture. The president of the Tom Huston Peanut Company of Columbus, Georgia, Tom Huston, later presented Carver a bas-relief of the latter as a mark of honor. This relief was deposited with Tuskegee Institute.

The other activities to which his genius extended are numerous: enrichment and diversification of beverages, mixed pickles, sauces, coffee, bleach, washing powder, metal polish, paper, ink, plastics, rubbing oil, axle grease, synthetic rubber, sweet potatoes, tapioca, molasses, dyes, starch, and flour. He was conversant with the uses of clay and how to make permanent colors. He found antidotes against cotton boll weevil and discovered the many uses of wild plants for food. As a renowned vegetarian he popularized hawk weeds, the giant thistle, black mustard, evening primrose, water grass, geraniums and many more too numerous to enumerate.

It suffices to state that his research revolutionized agricultural methods and led the way to new industries in the South. His precision at work and his patience were an inspiration to his followers and enhanced the belief in their possibilities of success. New factories were set up and employment created for thousands of workers, mostly of the black race. In addition, the George Washington Carver Foundation, established posthumously with his own bequest, carries on his scientific work at Tuskegee for the honor of his race and the service of humanity.

Carter Woodson's importance is as an innovator.[13] He was for many years the only voice of any consequence in black American historiography. He is largely responsible for the present-day reevaluation of the role of the Negro in American history and life.

Woodson was born in Virginia, in 1875, and received an extensive education at several of the finest universities both in the United States and abroad. Included among the institutions that he attended are Berea College, the University of Chicago, Harvard University, and the Sorbonne in Paris.

Woodson proved to be an effective and prolific organizer, as attested to by the success and number of organizations that he founded. His first major effort resulted in the establishment of the Association for the Study of Negro Life and History in Chicago in 1915. The purpose of this association was to save and publish the record of Negro achievement, so that the Negro would not become "a negligible factor in the thought of the world." In 1916 he founded the *Journal of Negro History,* a publication designed to carry out the aims of the Association for the Study of Negro Life and History. In 1921 he organized the Associated Publishers in order to produce textbooks and other materials about the black man, which at that time was not done by other publishers. In 1932 the *Negro History Bulletin* began producing issues under Woodson's guidance.

Woodson was active in education, teaching elementary and high school, and served as Dean of the School of Liberal Arts at Howard University. He also spent considerable time traveling extensively in Europe, Asia, and Africa.

In addition to editing the previously mentioned publications and doing considerable research and writing for them, he was the author of numerous books upon which contemporary historians have based much of their research. His most important books include *The Education of the Negro Prior to 1861* (1915), *A Century of Negro Migration* (1918), *The Negro in Our History*

(1922), *The Rural Negro* (1930), and *Negro Orators and Their Orations* (1925).

However, to list his exploits and actions as has been done above does not adequately describe his total contribution to his own race and the world. Woodson's ideals and beliefs are as important and relevant today as were his achievements in the past. He believed that the contribution of blacks would stand out well if the facts were presented honestly and dispassionately. He always maintained that there was one, and only one, history of the United States that all its citizens shared. His efforts, then, were a positive attempt to fill a void that had long existed and to demonstrate that the black race has an important place in the history of the United States. Woodson also realized that the white man had obscured and ignored the culture and civilization that had been achieved by the Africans before the Europeans arrived. Along with W. E. B. Du Bois, Woodson was the first historian to write about the black American within the context of African civilization. Others had seen blacks only from within a narrow American view, ignoring the black man's place of origin. Woodson felt it necessary to prove that Richard Wright spoke correctly when he said:

> We smelted iron, danced, made music, and recited folk poems; we sculptured, worked in glass, spun cotton and wool, wove baskets and cloth; we invented a medium of exchange; mined silver and gold, made pottery and cutlery; we fashioned tools and utensils of brass, bronze, ivory, quartz, and granite, we had our own literature, our own systems of law, religion, medicine, science, and education; we painted in color upon rocks; we raised cattle, sheep, and goats; we planted and harvested grain—in short, centuries before the Romans ruled, we lived as men.

Most of Woodson's life was spent fighting the idea of black inferiority and lack of accomplishment. He strove to balance the achievements of blacks, attempting to prevent underemphasis while guarding against overemphasis. His success is evident in the present-day awareness of the black past. Although numerous events have had some effect on the topic of awareness of the black past, it is doubtful that without Carter G. Woodson's efforts this awareness would be even approaching its present strength.

The history of the United States contains numerous instances of major contributions by blacks. This paper specifically has pointed out seven inventors and innovators whose achievements have been particularly important. However, this is not to say that other blacks have not contributed to the field of invention; it is increasingly evident as the facts of black history become more widely known that numerous blacks have had significant accomplishments. It is due to a variety of factors, most relating back to prejudice, that the achievements of black persons are only now becoming known.

BLACKS AS ORGANIZERS AND MANAGERS

Organizers and managers in business have been given the greatest attention in the study of entrepreneurship. They are the businessmen who provide capital for development or carry out the function of speculation and investment of the funds. They take risks, which many normal citizens will be loathe to do, in the hope of higher financial rewards. The organizers are able to perceive business opportunities and to initiate activities to take advantage of them. To this class belongs the Schumpetrian will to fight, to conquer, to achieve. These people possess splendid audacity and a vital energy, and the indomitable spirit to take chances and risks while facing uncertainty.

Managers on the other hand perform enterpreneurial functions—not only do they carry out the already laid down functions of the board governors or the organizers, but they have the capacity of innovation and can influence the pace and direction of economic activities.

While the social situation favored the whites—providing social, psychological, and economic incentives—the blacks in reverse were handicapped. To the agressiveness and dynamism of the former is matched the legal inhibitions and social opprobrium of the latter. Yet some progress was made. For illustrative purposes we shall select three leading black entrepreneurs in this category: Marcus Garvey, Asa Philip Randolph, and John H. Johnson.

Marcus Garvey[14]

Garvey's contribution to American economic history includes the wealth and variety of his ideas as well as his pioneering spirit and organizational abilities. The former has been dubbed utopian and the latter disastrous. Yet recent decades have seen such a revival of his ideas that a consideration of these in their historical background becomes necessary.

Born in Jamaica in 1887, Garvey spent the first fifteen years of his life in his home country. In 1912 he traveled to London where he was confronted by the plight of blacks coming from all over the British Commonwealth. He returned in 1914 and worked as a newspaper editor, where he expounded his vision of uniting all the black peoples of the world into one great body to establish a country and government absolutely their own. To promote this, he established, in 1914, the Universal Negro Improvement Association and the American Communities League under the motto, One God! One Aim! One Destiny! From this time on, he established a close contact with Booker T. Washington who had fairly similar but less radical views on blacks in business and social life.

A year later Garvey established a branch of the UNIA in Harlem and its membership rose from 1500 in two weeks to "several" million within five years. With his base here, he aimed at building the organization into a worldwide movement. One instrument he used to help spread his ideology was his newspaper, the *Negro World*, which was printed in English, French, and Spanish. Its circulation grew to a peak of 200,000, reaching the mass of blacks in many continents. A second instrument of propagation was the First Annual Convention of the UNIA, which met in New York for the first time in August 1920. This convention adopted a "Declaration of the Rights of the Negro

Peoples of the World," approved a flag for the movement, created a provisional government, and organized a massive march through Harlem. By the end of the convention, Garvey's movement had attracted worldwide attention.

With the growth in membership and a clearer definition of aims, the organization set out to establish a black nation in Liberia, which would stand as an example of success to the black people of the world. These plans were, however, shattered in 1924 when the Liberian government, under pressure by the French and the British, refused to grant the blacks land in Liberia on which they could establish their black nation. Along with defining future plans, the movement created an economic base of cooperation. The program included the Black Star Steamship Company, the Negro Factory Corporation, a commercial and industrial mission to Liberia, the Universal African Motor Corps, and various other auxiliary organs of the movement.

The Black Star Steamship Line was the major economic venture of the UNIA. In 1919 Garvey projected the idea of an all-Negro steamship company that would link the colored peoples of the world in commercial and industrial intercourse. This was a bold idea since it involved an invasion of the white-dominated maritime industry. Because of its boldness, the idea quickly gained the support of the members and for several months money was collected to purchase ships. In order to avoid legal difficulties, Garvey secured a broad charter of incorporation from the state of Delaware and under the charter of the Black Star Line "was explicitly authorized to own, charter, operate, and navigate ships of various types in any part of the world and to carry passengers, freight and mails." The B.S.L. was capitalized at $5 million, composed of one million shares of stock with a value of five dollars each. The advantages of the scheme were great. First, it helped build the idea of eventual separation from the United States, since transportation was now available. Second, it gave even the poorest black man a chance to become a stockholder in a big business enterprise. He was offered both the chance to make money and a chance to help his own race.

Sale of Black Star stock was limited to members of the black race, and no individual could purchase more than 200 shares. Cronon summarizes below some aspects of the venture:

> Ostensibly, the Black Star Line was established as a strictly commercial venture, and Garvey did not intend, as his critics sometimes claimed, that the line would merely be the vehicle for transportation of all Negroes back to their African homeland. The publicity value of the venture, however, far exceeded anything that it was likely to achieve commercially; and Garvey, always the master propagandist, skillfully exploited this aspect of the undertaking to the fullest extent.

A second major economic venture undertaken by Garvey was the establishment in 1919 of the Negro Factories Corporation, which was capitalized at $1 million, again in the state of Delaware. The purpose of the company in the *Negro World's* words was to build and operate factories in the big industrial centers of the United States, Central America, the West Indies, and Africa with the intent of manufacturing every marketable commodity. Blacks were told that their support of this venture would lead them to secure employment for their sons and daughters. The corporation developed a chain of cooperative grocery stores, a restaurant, a steamlaundry, a tailor and dressmaking shop, a millinery store, and a publishing house. However, as was seen in the case of the Black Star Line, the major emphasis was ideological rather than commercial. The same conclusion can be made about the various other commercial ventures of the UNIA. They were primarily designed to create group consciousness and racial solidarity. Economic cooperation was the medium rather than the goal.

The economic ventures of the UNIA all collapsed as a result of bad choice of enterprises and management. As they failed, criticism of Garvey grew in volume and intensity. A judge, considering the Black Star Line, told the investors, "You should have taken this $600,000 and built a hospital for colored people in the city rather than purchasing a few old boats." As public criticism grew, the judiciary increased its attack on Garvey and in 1923 he was convicted of mail fraud in connection with the Black Star Line. In 1925 he went to jail, and in 1927 he was deported to Jamaica. From there he went to London in 1934, where he died in 1940. Without its leader, the UNIA quickly disintegrated, its membership was soon lost, and the followers were attracted to new nationalist movements—the Black Muslims being the most successful in this regard.

What is the relevance of the above brief historical survey? The first lesson is that Garvey had economic ideas designed to build a separate black nation in Africa rather than within the United States. This meant that blacks were to be organized into a vanguard for Africa's redemption from colonialism, and this was to be achieved through economic cooperation. The second lesson is the psychological impact of Garveyism. Attempting to vindicate the leader, the *Spokesman* read, "Garvey made thousands think, who had never thought before. Thousands who merely dreamed dreams, now see visions." Garvey awakened the blacks to the realization that there was a possibility for the future if they became aware of their race and if they organized, even if it meant making inroads into the white man's economic domain.

Garvey's influence has been attested to even by the greatest critics. One of these, W. E. B. Du Bois, acclaimed him "an astonishing, popular leader, a master of propaganda." His popularity was due to the fact that he went into the heart of the race problem by hitting against the shame and inferiority that debilitated the development of the blacks. In another way, he was able to demonstrate the type of activities or organizations that could uphold the race. His ventures might now be lost but the philosophy of black economic independence, which Garvey fostered, is now reaching new levels of popularity.

Had Garvey succeeded in his undertakings, he would have been incontestably the greatest figure of the twentieth century. Having failed, he is considered utopian. In spite of the vehemence of criticisms against him, Garvey remains a shining example of black entrepreneurship, a man of ideas and vision, an indomitable organizer.

EXPLORATIONS IN
BLACK ENTREPRENEURIAL HISTORY

It augurs well for the future that there are among blacks of both sexes and all ages those who have given thought to the direction to which we must go. Still others whose inventions and innovations answered the call for new devices and others who carried out the task of organizing the factors of production for human welfare shout to be heard.

While this is good in itself, we should not ignore the difficulties in the way of discovering and of using our ideas. The American society, frequently sluggish, is constantly diversifying. Processes of work are multiplying daily—and so is division of labor. In the attempt to cope with the situation, we are confronted with an avalanche of new ideas and scientific formulations. What is the relevance of these to our topic? It is that our interests are easily ignored.

Asa Philip Randolph

Asa Philip Randolph was one of the most eminent Americans of the twentieth century. Born in 1889 in Crescent City, Florida, Randolph attended Bethune-Cookman College in Daytona Beach, Florida. He was a vice-president of the American Federation of Labor—Congress of Industrial Organizations (AFL-CIO), and he is credited with the organization of the Brotherhood of Sleeping Car Porters in 1925 and for being instrumental in the movement to cancel government contracts of industries that discriminated against blacks. His outspoken criticism of the discrimination that occurred in the armed forces of the U.S. influenced President Truman's decision to integrate the army.

Randolph was a master propagandist. Between 1917 and 1928, he edited the *Messenger* magazine, a publication that espoused the belief that the only way to solve black workers' problems was for them to unite with white labor. Randolph appealed to organized labor to admit blacks into their ranks and exhorted the former to join these unions. The *Messenger* was published in New York, where the socialist-oriented clothing trades and unions provided blacks with a unique opportunity for united black labor action and social advancement. However, the only real success of the *Messenger* was the organization of the Brotherhood of Sleeping Car Porters.

In January 1941, A. Philip Randolph, then president of the Brotherhood of Sleeping Car Porters, began to organize a march of black people on Washington, D.C. The reason for this massive rally was to protest the federal government's discriminatory hiring practices of blacks in American defense industries. Many federal officials viewed this march with much skepticism. Despite many personal and political attacks, Randolph went on to organize what most white Americans felt impossible. Soon his idea gained momentum and all segments of the black communities were involved. Thousands of black people throughout the United States prepared to march on the Capitol and White House on July 1, 1941. Finally, after much deliberation, Randolph and President Roosevelt agreed on a compromise, which involved the issuance of Executive Order 8802, stating that "there shall be no discrimination in the employment of workers in defense industries." Randolph's movement conclusively proved to black people that they did have a voice and that it could be heard.

Late in 1947, Randolph organized "The League of Non-Violent Civil Disobedience against Military Segregation." On March 22, 1948, he and a group of blacks met with President Truman at the White House. Randolph told the president, "Negroes are sick and tired of being asked to shoulder guns in defense of democracy abroad until they get some at home." The following week he testified before the Senate Armed Forces Committee: "I personally pledge myself to openly counsel, aid, and abet youth, both white and Negro, in an organized refusal to register and be drafted." Randolph and his followers did not argue that prejudice could be eliminated by law, but that it should not be allowed to deprive blacks of their constitutional rights as men and as citizens. Randolph's argument was chiefly concerned with legal rights. However, it went much deeper. Many blacks, especially war veterans of World War II, regarded it even more as a matter of outraged manhood and self-respect.

In Randolph's early days of protest, many conservative blacks felt that his position and proposals for ending racial segregation in the armed forces and industry would label the whole race as disloyal and reverse the trends of progress being made by a few blacks. Despite these misconceptions, Randolph continued his battle against racism, and though he occasionally suffered white "blacklash," he fought hard to make America safe for democracy. He led a strong opposition against whites who sought to impede the progress of black men in America; he moved to topple barriers keeping blacks out of war industries and the military, and his planned march on Washington was generally credited with the founding of the Fair Employment Practices Committee (FEPC). In the Spring of 1960, Randolph established the Negro American Labor Council (NALC) to fight discrimination from within the AFL-CIO. The (NALC) board consists of black members of unions and has affiliates throughout the United States. One of its most important functions has been organizing black caucuses within large, predominantly white labor unions. In 1963, a dramatic goal was reached with the election of a black man to the international board of the United Auto Workers (UAW).

Randolph was a valiant soldier struggling against the iniquities of racism in the United States at a time when many blacks were afraid to jeopardize themselves. He continued to introduce numerous resolutions against racial discrimination until his semiretirement. Unquestionably he was a major force in the organizational history of the black man in America. The system of industrial union clearly brought many blacks into the labor movement. Randolph was able to institute a new organizational power through constructive and effective means. He instituted, throughout the United States, actions that forced black people out of second-class citizenship.

John H. Johnson

Another black organizer to be considered as a major force in black economic history is John H. Johnson, president of the multimillion dollar Johnson Publishing Company in Chicago.

Johnson owns and dominates the nation's only black publishing enterprise in the United States. In addition, he owns a cosmetics company and is chairman of the board of Supreme Life Insurance Company, probably the largest black insurance business concern in the North. His publishing company has made him potentially one of the most powerful men in American society.

Johnson's road to success has probably been much tougher than most millionaires in the United States because as a black man he has had to fight in a business climate dominated by whites. His largest asset is *Ebony* magazine, a monthly peridoical devoted to news about black people throughout the world. In June of 1967, the circulation of *Ebony* passed the one million mark and earned $7 million in revenues from advertising. It has continued to grow as both blacks and whites subscribe. His other publications include *Jet,* a pocket-size weekly; *Tan,* a confession magazine; and *Black World* (formerly *Negro Digest*), a pubication that consists of serious articles and short stories by black authors.

Johnson maintains that the key to his success with *Ebony, Jet,* and *Tan* has been his ability to persuade white advertisers that black people represent an untapped market that he can help them tap. Johnson's belief is epitomized by this statement: "The Black market is a basic market, defined, precisely, by its exclusions from the white market." In his optimism he predicts that *Ebony* will eventually compete successfully with white magazines for the general reading audience. On the other hand, his argument to the white advertisers is that black people regard *Ebony* as their magazine. Johnson's argument does have merit. For purposes of illustration, every year black organizations throughout the United States sponsor subscription drives in order to increase the circulation of *Ebony.* But not all people, including blacks, regard him with such fervor. He has been accused as a mere tool of the white establishment's exploitation of black people. *Ebony,* it is argued, has failed to lead the aspirations of black people. Poor blacks and politically conscious blacks believe that *Ebony* reflects a middle-class orientation that does an injustice to black liberation.

Johnson's rise to fame and fortune began with a high school speech in the spring of 1936. He was one of two members of his graduation class of Chicago's predominantly black Du Sable High School to be recognized at the honors convocation exercises. His speech, entitled "America's Challenge to Youth," caught the attention of the featured speaker of the day, Harry H. Pace, then president of Supreme Life Insurance Company. After a short meeting with Mr. Pace, Johnson decided that he would attend the University of Chicago part time and support himself by working at Supreme Life as an office boy. During these years at Supreme Life, Johnson gained experience in business and finance.

In 1939 while working at Supreme, he decided to take a brief fling into the realm of politics. He became part-time secretary to Earl Dickerson, an idealistic young lawyer. Johnson's job was to help draft ordinances against restrictive covenants in property deeds and do research on slum housing. However, reform was not yet a significant cause, and in 1943 Dickerson was defeated, and Johnson soon lost interest in politics.

His initiation in publishing came when he mortgaged his mother's furniture for five hundred dollars to pay for postage for 20,000 letters to Supreme's customers offering a charter subscription to *Negro Digest*. In 1945, he launched *Ebony* "to emphasize the brighter side of black life and success." After six months he announced that the magazine would accept advertising. But the response to the announcement was very small. Only after writing letters and pleading with company executives did he persuade them to advertise in *Ebony*. Soon he was successful. Johnson's other publications, *Tan* and *Jet*, were started in 1950 and 1951, respectively. *Jet* is a new magazine concentrating on stars, actresses, and some sensationalism, while *Tan* is basically a confession magazine.

Johnson believed that young blacks with talent and ambition should attempt to become self-employed and entrepreneurially oriented, rather than seek entrance in the white-oriented world of corporate business.

A history of black entrepreneurship is illuminating in furnishing the reader with valuable information on blacks like W. E. B. Du Bois, Booker T. Washington, and Malcolm X, men whose ideas changed economic life and whose economic philosophies have relevance for their times and for later generations.

Similarly, many black inventors and innovators left decided footprints on the economic landmarks of the nation. In this chapter, we have been able to illustrate this fact and to fill a gap in American history by touching upon a few people of innovative abilities. There are others, to be sure, such as Madame Walker, Elijah Muhammad, and Benjamin Mays who made contributions in organization and management.

Human Capital Formation: The Role of Black Educators and Educational Institutions

INTRODUCTION

Four main functions can be assigned to the role of education in the formation of the human potential.[1] The first is the supply of skilled manpower and technicians that will maximize physical capital of all kinds. The second is the generation of a climate for growth. By this is meant that education gives the masses a capacity for thinking beyond their present occupations and thus enables them to foresee the future needs and aspirations of the society and their implications. Where this is true, we can expect the emergence of entrepreneurs and pioneers. The third is the furnishing of elementary skills with which natural resources can be turned to more productive uses. The higher the level of education, the higher will be the rate of growth of the economy. To the above economic-oriented functions is added a fourth, namely, the capacity for education to yield the opportunities for appropriating more advantageously the intangible "life's chances" like leisure and intellectual pursuits. Education helps the beneficiary to acquire the appropriate habits of thought and expression and the skills to affect and organize more effectively nature's endowments and man's welfare.

While the first three can be called the economics of education, the last is the cultural component. In the history of education, the last has always been regarded as the most important. Education was meant to train culturally emancipated citizens, distinguished in appropriate manners and decent modes of speech and dress. In recent times, however, the economic functions have received a great emphasis and closer scrutiny. Of immediate concern to us is the question, Who determines what is good for the individual's education? In the case of blacks we can distinguish four categories of people or groups who influenced or directed the trend of black education: 1) the proponents of higher education that would be liberal and extensive rather than narrow and vocational—the leading figure of this school of thought being W. E. B. Du Bois; 2) the school of thought emphasizing the acquisition of technical skills for economic success and the cultivation of good manners—Booker T. Washington best typifying this school of thought; 3) those who consider education for blacks to be religious and technical, teaching good habits of thought, expression, and behavior and imparting skills that could be used in industries—a view accepted by many northern whites; and 4) those who wanted an educational system that kept blacks servile as doemstic hands and as unskilled workers— the view accepted by many southern whites.

The Proponents of Higher Education

Throughout the past century there were black leaders who advocated higher education. This was significant, particularly in the late nineteenth century, when higher education even among whites was the luxury of a few. Yet at those times strong pleas were made by black leaders for the provision of educational and intellectual opportunities. In this section we shall discuss a few of these personalities.

The dominant nationalist ideologies in the past, as of today, were race pride, race solidarity and unity, support for black business, and colonization. In the achievement of these, many leaders like Alexander Crummell, Francis J. Grimke, Arthur A. Schomburg, Carter G. Woodson, and W. E. B. Du Bois believed that the black college graduate had a special role to play in elevating the race and bringing it to its rightful position of respect, wealth, and power.

As early as the 1890s Alexander Crummell, one of the founders of the American Negro Academy, called attention to the special role of the black elite in the civilization of the race. In a report of 1897, he said, among other things:

> For the creation of a complete and rounded man, you need the impress and the moulding of the highest arts. But how much more so for the realizing of a true and lofty race of men. What is true of a man is deeply true of a people. The special need in such a case is the force and application of the highest arts, not mere mechanization, not mere machinery, not mere temporal ambitions. These are but incidents; important indeed, but pertaining mainly to man's material needs, and to the feeding of the body. And the incidental in life is incapable of feeding the soul.[2]

Crummell pleaded for the development of men, not material wealth, and for the vitalizing qualities that alone could lift his people.[3] Who were to be the agents to do this and to "bring up to the height of noble thought, grand civility, a chaste and elevating culture, refinement, and the impulses of irrepressible progress," he asked. They were black scholars and thinkers, those who had secured the vision of nature, studied the history of civilization, and those who knew the best methods of effecting changes in the society. Only those who possessed intelligence, said Crummell, could transform and stimulate the souls of a race. Since every man cannot be a philosopher, only a few qualified for this role. In order for the race to survive, it was therefore imperative, he said, that a cadre of trained and scholarly men of the race should be developed, for to them alone belongs the capacity of moulding the opinions and habits of the masses and of guiding them.

It is significant that Crummell qualifies his view by adding that the black elite had to be philanthropists in order to be reformers, for, he maintained, without duty, leadership was meaningless. Without responsibility "then with all their Latin

and Greek and science they are but pedants, trimmers, oppor-
tunists."

Crummell was not alone in his view. Around the same time,
Francis J. Grimke, while welcoming the growing institutions of
higher learning for blacks, insisted that their role was not only
the education of the young, but the maintenance of scholarship,
the development of research, and the instilling of race pride and
mutual respect. White professors, he claimed, were unsuitable in
doing this, and the shutting out of black professors twenty years
after emancipation (at a time when "on the list of graduates
from our leading institutions—Harvard, Yale, Dartmouth,
Amherst, Brown, Oberlin—are to be found representatives of
our race") was a disservice to the black race. Only opportunity
could enable the black professor to prove his worth and to serve
his race.

By the turn of the century, Arthur A. Schomburg was advocating the creation of chairs of Negro History.[4] Schomburg
declared that this plea was not to revolutionize but to improve
and amend existing standards. Oral history, he said, in which the
history of blacks was steeped, was worthy of study. But it needed
the application of trained minds. Books by white authors, great
and small, were to be found in white libraries, but not so with
black authors, Schomburg maintained. He regretted the non-
popularization of the works of writers like Philis Wheatley, the
poetess, George M. Horton, author of *Praises of Creation,* Islay
Walden, the blind poet of North Carolina, Francis E. Watkins,
David Walker, and—not the least—the slave narratives of John
Brown, William Wells Brown, Frederick Douglass, and Samuel
Ringgold. These and many more, he said, deserved a place of
honor in college libraries. In his frustration and impatience
Schomburg declared:

> We have chairs of almost everything, and believe we lack nothing,
> but we sadly need a chair of Negro history. The white institutions
> have their chair of history; it is the history of their people, and
> whenever the Negro is mentioned in the textbooks it dwindles
> down to a footnote.[5]

The black race, in his view, needed teachers and philosophers, historians and writers to "give us the background to our future" and "the story of our forefathers" who smelted iron and tempered bronzes at a time when Europe was wielding stone implements; who knew the arts of writing, which Europe imported and later shipped to America. And should these historians lack style, Schomburg concluded, the rising generation of blacks should "correct the omission of their sires."

It is noteworthy how, in the above studies, we hear reechoed the need for men of letters and research, who with their training could add a new dimension to American society. Education here is to serve another purpose, that of discovering the past, which serves as the basis of pride. Frederick Douglass, in one of his orations, contended, however, that pride of achievement was to be preferred to race pride. For him only personal achievement gave reason for pride.[6] "If black people were to be proud," he said, "let it be because we have had some agency in producing that of which we can properly be proud." While not disparaging Douglass, it must be emphasized that pride of achievement and race pride are intertwined and hardly distinguishable. The knowledge of the achievements of the race give pride that is shared by all individuals in the society. The study of black history opens this avenue.

A great advocate of black scholarship was Carter G. Woodson, whom we have already discussed. It suffices here to add that with the founding of the Association for the Study of Negro Life and History, he projected the training of researchers in the social sciences and for instruction in colleges and universities.

No doubt, the best-known protagonist of higher, liberal education for the black American is Dr. W. E. B. Du Bois. His educational philosophy is predictated upon the role he believed blacks had to play in the American society. In many ways this role conformed to the aims of education mentioned earlier, but specifically it is illustrated in an address he delivered in 1897 to the American Negro Academy entitled "The Conservation of Races":

. . . that if in America it is to be proven for the first time in the modern world that not only are Negroes capable of evolving individual men like Toussaint, the Saviour, but are a nation stored with wonderful possibilities of culture, then their destiny is not servile imitation of Anglo-Saxon culture, but a stalwart originality which shall unswervingly follow Negro ideals.[7]

To Du Bois it is the role of the black race and particularly its scholarly men and women to

strive in every honorable way for the realization of the best and highest aims, for the development of strong manhood and pure womanhood, and for the rearing of a race ideal in America, to the glory of God and the uplifting of the Negro people.[8]

In the formulation of his notion of leadership, the college-educated elite is regarded as of vital importance. This percentile of the race, or in Du Bois' words, the "Talented Truth"—the choicest brains in the black community—are those who through their scholarship and personal achievements not only instill race pride but will lead the black masses out of poverty and ignorance.[9]

Du Bois believed that higher education would train the manhood of the black nation in the knowledge of the world and that this education was utilitarian as well as intellectual. In other words, his educational philosophy sought to combine utilitarianism or relevance and practical usefulness with intellectualism or what he called a "broad cultural life." The latter should from then on receive greater attention since, in his view, the former need was being met by Tuskegee and similar schools. Industrial and vocational education, he maintained, was excellent as long as it did not exclude others or arrogate preeminence to itself. Du Bois urged blacks to become dissatisfied with vocationalism lest it restrict the nation to perpetual semiskilled jobs and thus to a lower status in the society.

Du Bois' educational program was the selection of children of ability and genius and their encouragement by the best and most exhaustive training, so that they would supply the community and the world with leaders, thinkers, and artists. This training should, he insisted, be done in all institutions at home and abroad, but in doing this, preference should be given to black institutions, which are necessary for "positive advance and negative defense." Du Bois further believed that the attempt of whites to keep the elite as well as the mass of the black race shut off from higher education would eventually lead to the economic ruin of the whites. Liberal education for blacks was therefore the answer to an intelligent participation in the American political and economic processes.

The Proponents of Technical and Vocational Education

The most dominant philosophy of the education of blacks until the 1950s had been technical and vocational training. The major advocates were whites but numerous blacks were included as supporters of this view. The origin of technical education can be traced to the handicraft and artisan workshops of the slavery period. In essence, it conformed to the Puritan ethical and economic teachings of training the individual in the acquisition of manual skills and the respect for labor.

Attributes claimed for this form of education were the cultivation of habits of thrift, self-help, industry, economic independence and morality; the acquisition of skills and the transformation of concrete objects for school and factory uses; the opening of the avenue of material success and the eventual achievement of a higher and honorable status in the society. Finally, as seen by some whites, technical and vocational education served to adjust the craftsman to his subordinate and lowly status in the society.

Frederick Douglass[10] and Booker T. Washington[11] argued for their educational philosophies from a fundamental conviction about black destiny. Douglass, a believer in racial harmony and assimilation, held that the best contribution blacks could make to the American society was to participate in industry.

Like Booker T. Washington later, Douglass believed that higher education was for the select few. A developing economic force needed practical things, as opposed to "superfluous skills, such as Greek or Latin." He concluded that "one must train the hand, before the head." As Douglass put it years before:

> What can be done to improve the condition of the free colored people in the United States? The plan which I humbly submit in answer to this inquiry . . . is the establishment . . . of an *Industrial College*, in which shall be taught several important branches of the mechanical arts. . . . The fact is . . . that colored men must learn trades . . . or that they must decay under the present wants to which their condition is rapidly bringing them. We must become mechanics . . . before we can properly live, or be respected by our fellow men. . . . It must be confessed that the most powerful argument, now used by the Southern slaveholders and the one most soothing to his conscience . . . is that derived from the low condition of the free colored people at the North. I have long felt that too little attention has been given, by our truest friends in this country, to removing this stumbling block out of the way of the slaves' liberation.[12]

In a similar vein, Booker T. Washington regarded industrial education as the only form of education suitable to the illiterate and impoverished freedmen. Rather than go for higher education or rush for political power, blacks should spend time learning skills, acquiring good habits of thrift and respect for labor. Intelligent management of farms, ownership of land, proficiency in mechanics, domestic services, and similar services were to be the pursuit of blacks if they were to survive.

Washington's speech at The Atlanta Exposition in 1895 summarized the above philosophy:

> Our greatest danger is that in the great leap from slavery to freedom we may overlook the fact that the masses of us are to live by the productions of hands, and fail to keep in mind that we shall prosper in proportion as we learn to dignify and glorify common labor and put brains and skill into the common occupations of life. . . . It is life. . . . It is at the bottom of life we must begin, and not at the top.

He established the Tuskegee Institute and strove thereby to enable blacks to rule out "certain unrealistic notions" that they had about their place in American society and to make them administer to the needs of an industrial society. Accommodation to the given society was the objective, and industrial education was the vehicle. Washington's model served as a compromise between the various views held by whites in the North and South and by the blacks themselves. There were fewer things on which the majority of the three groups agreed so much in the later nineteenth and the early twentieth centuries as on industrial education. Because of this, it was conveniently used by Washington to win financial support from whites in both North and South. Thus southern goodwill and northern philanthropy were bought with the industrial education package.

To further the above ideas, different schools were established, chief of which were the manual colleges, domestic science institutions, agricultural and mechanical universities and trade schools. As early as 1862, the first example of a land-grant college —the Morrit land-grant college—was established for blacks. These, and the Freedmen's Bureau and Mennonite school teachers, lent the program considerable support. The more the industrial revolution with its startling innovations in science and technology developed, the greater the impetus industrial education received and thence the greater the financial encouragement given for it.

The main subjects taught were sewing, shoemaking, household arts, janitorial work, domestic training, gardening, bricklaying, masonry, firework, carpentry, blacksmithing, wagonmaking, cabinetmaking, farming, and animal husbandry. As this list indicates, these were handicraft rather than industrial subjects, and it is therefore not surprising that those who were so trained left the trades for other employments or found themselves unemployable in the new and changing industrialism because their skills were simply unsuitable for competition in the industrial age. In the industrial universities the subjects taught were typical. Schools like Tougaloo College and Spelman Seminary, though specializing in elementary industrial education, began by the mid 1890s and early 1900s to add advanced studies in their curriculum, namely, nursing, mechanical courses, elementary engineering, advanced carpentry, printing, and steampower sawing.

In concluding this section we should observe that the two schools of thought were hardly in agreement as to the aims and programs of education for blacks. The controversy between them has been ably documented though unfortunately exaggerated by other writers. What can be said here is that the advocates of higher education were pressing for the ultimate, while the industrial education school of thought strove for the immediate.

The views of northern and southern whites are implicit in those of Booker T. Washington. By advocating industrial education they hoped to put the black man "in his place" and thereby reduce competition for the rising poor whites. In the same way skilled blacks would provide a ready source of labor for industries and thereby assure a regular and steady income to their promoters.

Each school of thought is the product of its time and the lives of its proponents. Industrial education was linked with the status of whites, but it had a symbolic value for blacks. None of the views on education worked out exactly as their proponents had forecast. As the American economy progressed, the education of blacks in both the professional and the technical fields was accepted as a political imperative.

In the remaining sections we shall discuss the history and assess the contribution of educational institutions toward the achievement of the above goals of education for blacks.

Problems and Prospects of Education

In colonial America, plantation owners saw to it that their slaves were taught just enough to make them obedient citizens and for this, Bible knowledge and the practice of Christian principles were emphasized. When slavery became an economic proposition, planters frowned on education for slaves and various states passed laws prohibiting it. The reasons for the opposition were obvious. There was the fact that property owners did not want to be taxed for the education of the poor. Also, poor whites were apathetic in educating their own children. For example, less than one-half of poor whites in Virginia attended schools in 1851. But even then those who did go to school completed only eleven weeks of the year. As would be expected, this attitude affected blacks as well. Another reason was that the education of slaves was feared as it made them dissatisfied with their lot, enabling them to desert their masters.

During this period few blacks received formal education. Men like John Brown Russwurm (1799-1851), reputed to be the first black college graduate in the country, and John Chavis, a free North Carolinian educated in Princeton, were the few exceptions to the general rule.

The end of the Civil War brought a movement for black education. Everywhere the thirst for education was great. The few existing facilities were not available to blacks and the government established the Freedmen's Bureau in 1865 to foster educational change. The bureau provided an impetus for black education. Northern philanthropists and churches sent financial assistance. Federal soldiers stayed in the South to be teachers, and the New England schools sent teachers to help the freedmen. Blacks did not lag behind in the promotion of their own education. Their initial efforts were mostly in the area of vocational and industrial education in the 1880s and less in the higher and liberal. But the masses showed a strong determination to learn and, once they had learned, to teach others.

Several individuals showed considerable enthusiasm in establishing schools. Fanny Jackson started the Coppin-Philadelphia Institute for Colored Youth. Lucy Laney built the Haines Normal and Industrial Institute in Augusta, Georgia (1886), and J. C. Price started the Livingstone College in South Carolina. Through various local churches, blacks pulled their resources together for the uplifting of their race.

Various missionary bodies had pioneered higher education for blacks before the Civil War but this trend gained momentum with the establishment of the Freedmen's Bureau. The missionary bodies most active in promoting education and the institutions they either established or supported were: the Presbyterians (Ashmun Institute, 1852, renamed Lincoln University, 1866) ; the Methodists (Wilberforce University, Tawawa Springs, Ohio, 1856) ; the United Presbyterians (Knoxville College, Tennessee, 1875) ; the African Methodist Episcopal Church (which later acquired Wilberforce University and established Western University in Kansas in 1864, Allen University in Columbia, South Carolina, 1881, and Morris Brown University in Atlanta, 1886) ; the Colored Methodist Church (Lane College in Jackson, Tennessee, 1882) ; and the American Missionary Association (Hampton Institute, Virginia, 1868, and Tuskegee Institute, Alabama, 1868).

Other agencies of importance were the federal government (Howard University, 1867) and the Morril Fund, 1862, for agricultural and mechanical colleges (Hampton Institute; Clafin College, South Carolina; Alcorn A&M College, 1878). Some foundations that also helped were the Rockefeller Foundation, the John I. Slater Fund (1882), the P. Carnegie Foundation for the Advancement of Teaching, the United States Bureau of Education, and the Phelps-Stokes Fund.

Educational Institutions and High-Level Manpower Training[13]

The major obstacle confronting the effort in the attainment of full citizenship in the United States today is economic inequality. The removal of unfair employment practices alone does not necessarily lead to a high increase in the number employed, at least not in the higher levels of management. Equal opportunity denotes at the same time equal education and experience. For the employment of blacks to increase there has to be an attitudinal change within the labor market. Certainly, educational competence must complement the elimination of discrimination if equal opportunity is to become a reality. The entrance to most sectors of the higher echelons of industry and administration is predicated upon the attainment of a college education or its equivalent. The history of black educational institutions is a clear indication of the efforts to train persons for high-level positions.

Let us now take a look at a few black colleges for purposes of illustration. We shall discuss their growth, problems, and achievements in this respect. In this study we shall deal with Howard, Hampton, Fisk, and Tuskegee, thus including the main divisions of black education—technical and liberal—which are to be regarded as the two sides of the same blade and not necessarily as competitive or exclusive approaches.

Between 1860 and 1865 education was pioneered by northern benevolent missionary bodies and the major emphasis was on elementary education. The period 1886-1928 witnessed a shift of emphasis to the secondary and higher education. The general pattern of the classical colleges influenced the majority of the institutions.

Between 1917 and 1928 several philanthropic foundations joined in promoting higher education after the publication of a *Survey on Black Education* made by the Phelps-Stokes Fund and the United States Bureau of Education. This report underscored the need for supporting black education. The period since 1928 is one of consolidation, in which black educational institutions made efforts to satisfy accreditation requirements following the Phelps-Stokes Fund Survey.

The least number of black colleges came before the Civil War and most of them had religious beginnings or influence. For example, Lincoln University was charted in 1862 as Ashmun Institute and aimed at training ministers and missionaries for Africa. The same objective was true of Wilberforce University in Ohio and other famous institutions like Atlanta, Fisk, Shaw, and Morehouse. Some of these colleges began their "higher" work on a very low base and in humble places such as abandoned Union army barracks, damp basements in small churches, rented halls, teachers' homes, and even a boxcar!

It was not only the humble beginnings that affected the quality of education but also the models and patterns of education itself. Undoubtedly imitation or an importation of models could ruin an educational structure or at least lead to a wastage of resources. This is seen in the admission requirements of the black colleges that were patterned after those of the dominant white colleges and universities. This, in view of pedagogical and social differences, meant wastage rates, since the type of education was not attuned to the peculiar socio-economic needs and circumstances of blacks as was the case for whites. What were these entrance requirements? They were generally: two books of Caesar, six orations of Cicero, the Bucolics, six books of Vergil's *Aeneid,* Sallust's *Cataline,* two books of Xenophon's *Anabasis,* and the first books of Homer's *Illiad.* And the result? A small initial enrollment in black colleges. In order to increase enrollment, black educators began preparing their freshmen from the elementary grades within their own institutions. Clearly what was missing in that early formula were those requirements that could have built a base for black psychological strength and self-respect. The essence of African history, for example, reflected the sterility that had been inherited from white colleges.

THE PROGRESS OF SOME INSTITUTIONS

One of the most important institutions of higher learning was Howard University located in the nation's capital, Washington, D.C. By a charter granted it in 1867 by the federal government, the university aimed at providing for the education of youth in the liberal arts and sciences, without discrimination as to race. The curriculum included preparatory college work, theological training, business, and music. Complete courses in medicine, dentistry, and pharmacy were added a few years later. Howard has since added a School of Communication, School of Education, and a Banking Institute. President James Check has been credited with moving Howard out of a mediocre stage into a university of quality.

Another institution was Hampton founded in 1868 by

General Samuel Armstrong. Hampton Institute was the first missionary effort in the education of the freedmen. General Armstrong expressed the philosophy of the school as one to instill in the students a high regard for the dignity of labor and to impart the knowledge with which the youth would go out and teach and lead their people by example to acquire land and homes and to be self-reliant. It was to this end, Armstrong hoped, that the school could build up an industrial system, for the sake not only of self-support and intelligent labor, but also for the sake of character.

When Hampton opened in April 1868, it listed as its assets "two teachers, fifteen students, no money, and little equipment." Its principal, General Armstrong, a twenty-seven-year-old brevet brigadier general, was the son of missionaries. He was assigned by the Freedmen's Bureau to help solve the problems of the recently emancipated slaves. During these early days the admission standards were simple: sound health, good character, age not less than fourteen or over twenty-four, ability to do long division, and preparedness to remain the whole three years and to become a teacher. Hampton Institute gained early support from philanthropic and religious groups, from the Federal Land-Grant Funds (1872-1920), and, of course, from the Freedman's Bureau.

Academically, courses leading to the Bachelor of Science degree were first offered at Hampton in 1922. Then elementary and secondary levels were dropped. Accreditation as a class "A" college came in 1932-33. Hampton Institute is today a co-educational, privately supported college, providing specific vocational training through courses leading to the bachelor's degree, which are offered in the academic division of Architecture, Business, Fine Arts, Home Economics, Language and Literature, Mathematics and Natural Sciences, Nursing, Social Sciences, and Teacher Education. Hampton's Division of Graduate Studies offers a program leading to Master of Arts degree. It is a member of the Southern Association of Colleges and Schools and is accredited by the Department of Education of the Commonwealth of Virginia. Furthremore, the curriculum has been approved by the

University of the State of New York, and it is a member of the Association of American Colleges and the American Council on Education.

Fisk was established in 1866 and was dedicated to a liberal arts education and to the development of a broad understanding of the basic principles and values in the social sciences and humanities. It aimed further at instilling creativity in its students as well as giving them the advantages of a Christian education. Enrollment was open to all races. Like most black colleges it passed through the stages of high school and normal school before becoming a fully accredited liberal arts college. In 1930, it also became the first black college to gain accreditation by the Southern Association of Colleges and Schools. In 1933, it became the first of such colleges to be placed on the approval lists of the Association of American Universities and the American Association of University Women in 1952.

Fisk University's program is organized into two administrative units—the Basic College and the College of Higher Studies. The former is devoted to general education, while the latter is concerned with specialized instruction and research. The Basic College, furthermore, provides the main work during the freshman and sophomore years and offers a three-year program in general education for students. It aims at helping students master the tools of college writing, intelligent reading, logical and creative thinking and judgment. The curriculum of the Basic College includes courses in English, Humanities, Philosophy, Mathematics, Speech Communication, Natural Sciences, Modern Foreign Languages, and the Social Sciences. The rationale for this structure is that it enables a student, at the beginning of his junior year, to concentrate in his field of interest.

The College of Higher Studies provides specialized instruction and research leading to the B.A., B.S., and M.A. degrees. This division is comprised of seventeen major instructional areas, grouped in four units: 1) Social Sciences, 2) Natural Sciences, 3) Humanities, and 4) Physical Education. Upon entering the College of Higher Studies, each student must choose a field of concentration from these four units. Graduate instruction is offered in the College of Higher Studies in seven major areas: Chemistry, Education, Music, Physics, Psychology, Religion, and Sociology.

Tuskegee Institute in Alabama was established in 1881 under the leadership of Booker T. Washington to provide normal education for Afro-American teachers. Washington's aims were to give students an opportunity to learn "the correct habits of living," moral and religious ideals, respect for law, property accumulation and thrift, inasmuch as the development of these qualities was regarded an important element in the process of building white respect for black people, and hence in the improvement of black participation in the American economy. Another goal of the Institute was the inculcation of respect for manual labor as a countermeasure to its contempt, which slavery had produced, noticeable in the fact that blacks coming to college after the Civil War had hoped to pursue purely academic subjects. Through a combination of classroom education and field work, Washington attempted to correct this tendency and to correlate textbook knowledge with the needs of daily life.

Tuskegee education prepared the blacks for employment within the positions then available but hitherto untouched by them because of their lack of technical skills. The courses of instruction changed with time to reflect the changing needs of the people and the American economy. In 1891, instruction was offered in nineteen different trades. A Nurse's Training Course was added and a School of Home Economics opened. In addition, a night school was established for those who could not pay as day students. The training of teachers was pursued with vigor and zest.

Several public services were performed by Tuskegee Institute. Leadership in the organization of the National Negro Business League came from Tuskegee leaders beginning with Washington himself. Through the Instiute's conferences and distribution of literature, black business endeavors were aided. The Institute was a guide and an inspiration to the economic pursuits of local black farmers and workers. Tuskegee established a "Movable School" to introduce methods of scientific farming in an effort to improve the quality and quantity of agricultural products. With Hampton, it sponsored a National Negro Health Week for the improvement of health conditions among Southern blacks. Communications as a means of acquainting the blacks with developments in the nation was stressed by the Institute. True to its ideals of black-white cooperation as formulated by the founder, the Institute formed a Commission on Interracial Cooperation and conducted goodwill tours to improve race relations.

The influence of both Hampton and Tuskegee has been far-reaching. Many later-developed institutions of higher learning patterned themselves after these two schools. The grant colleges designated "A" and "M" (agricultural and mechanical) are examples of this influence. Though it could be said that the training limited blacks to certain manual jobs in the American labor market, it cannot be gainsaid that they filled a gap that no other institutions in their time were capable of closing. Nor was their training so limited as one so apt to think at first glance. Teacher training, carpentry, printing, nursing, and construction works were professional types of training equipping students to lead full and useful lives. Since 1927 certain courses have been upgraded to degree levels. In reality, many of the college graduates have not been confined to their trades since leaving school. They have gravitated into occupations where their versatile education prepared them. The fault of most of these colleges, however, was the inability to place self-knowledge on a par with skill acquisition.

Yet they have made a striking, if modest, contribution to the nation's high-level manpower. A rising trend is observable all along. In 1914, there were only 60 graduates from northern colleges and 559 graduates from black colleges. However, between 1920 and 1933 the number of black graduates from white colleges increased from 494 to 2,486 or 400 percent. During the years 1934-36, due to the economic depression and the difficulty in obtaining complete reports of graduates for those years, a marked decline appeared evident. Of the 43,821 black graduates, 37,397 or 85.5 percent graduated from black colleges between 1826-1936.

Of the degrees conferred, 70.9 percent were academic and 29.1 percent were professional. During the 1930s public support for higher education of blacks increased rather slowly. Consequently, the average incomes of those colleges were also low.

By 1937-38 three-quarters of all black college students were attending land-grant institutions. In 1940, enrollment at Fisk was 447. Fisk offered B.A.s and M.A.s in business, science, and teaching; Howard's enrollment during the same period was 1,232, and it offered B.A.s and M.A.s in liberal arts, architecture, business, dentistry, engineering, home economics, law, journalism, medicine, music, pharmacy, science, social science, teaching, and theology. These institutions have grown to become two of the major centers for the training of black professionals and leaders. Among other major institutions for training black professionals are state supported schools like Southern University, the largest predominantly black university in the world; Texas Southern; and Tennessee State University.

In spite of great handicaps and inadequate financial support, which affects equipment, library, and staffing, black colleges and universities have spearheaded the training of black high-level manpower. From initially concentrating on preachers and teachers, the schools have entered other professional fields, like medicine, law, and architecture, and have made Du Bois' dream of cultivating leaders a reality.

Blacks and Self-Help Organizations

MUTUAL AID AND SECRET SOCIETIES

The emergence of mutual aid and secret societies coincided with the emancipation and the weakness of the state apparatus to deal with the social and economic problems attendant on emancipation. In their origins the mutual aid and secret societies were closely connected with religious organizations, which provided the moral and financial support needed for their activities.

The main characteristics of the societies were three-fold: aid to members in time of sickness and death, concentration in rural areas, and the embodiment of elements of savings and insurance. In general they were set up to meet the harsh conditions of the rising industrialism in the North. Between 1787 and 1850, there were over 110 such societies, the most important of which were the Free African Society, which originated in Philadelphia in 1787, and the Brown Fellowship Society, which began in Charleston, South Carolina in 1790.

Secret Societies, on the other hand, antedated emancipation. In their constitutions they bore the imprint of European and African cultural backgrounds. The leading secret societies before and after emancipation were:

1. The Masonic Order (Boston), 1775. This was converted in 1787 to the African Lodge Number 459, after it was recognized by the Grand Lodge of England.

2. The Odd Fellows were first established in New York and later formed the Philomathean Lodge, also in New York, in 1843.
3. Negro Odd Fellows in Pennsylvania and Connecticut.
4. The Galilean Fishermen and the Nazarites in Baltimore arose shortly before the Civil War (1856).
5. The Samaritans and the Seven Wise Men, also in Baltimore.
6. The International Order of Twelve of the Knights and Daughters of Tabor, Independence, Missouri, 1871.
7. The Grand United Order of True Reformers. This Order is particularly important for pioneering in insurance, banking, and real estate among blacks.
8. The Independent Order of Good Samaritans and Daughters of Samaria were established in 1847. This was a temperance and relief society.
9. The Colored Knights of Pythias, Vicksburg, Mississippi, 1880.
10. The Mosaic Templars of America, 1882.
11. The Seven Sisters, New Orleans.

FRATERNAL ORGANIZATIONS

Special "sickness" societies with strong religious backgrounds, which met the needs of rural populations, arose after emancipation. They could be regarded as benevolent, charitable, or fraternal organizations, like the "Sons and Daughters of Esther," the "Brothers and Sisters of Charity," and the "Brothers and Sisters of Love." Other extensively organized fraternal organizations included the Colored Order of Elks (1889) in Cincinnati, which engaged in real estate and securities investment among urban dwellers. The Order of the Elks had the widest appeal among the rising middle-class blacks. Its programs cover the promotion of education, legal protection, health, and social welfare.

Black college campuses spawned Greek letter societies emphasizing intellectual and professional excellence, the maintenance of contacts among educated blacks in and outside the colleges, emancipation of black womanhood, and the promotion of socially desirable projects. Some of the more important societies have been:

1. Sigma Pi Phi Fraternity, Philadelphia, 1904.
2. Alpha Phi Alpha Fraternity, Cornell University, 1905-06.
3. Omega Psi Phi Fraternity, Howard University, 1911.
4. Phi Beta Sigma Fraternity, Howard University, 1914.
5. Kappa Alpha Psi Fraternity, University of Indiana, 1911.
6. The Alpha Kappa Alpha Sorority for Women, Howard University, 1908.
7. The Delta Sigma Theba Sorority, Howard University, 1913.

These college societies followed the examples of similar white organizations on campuses. They acted as rallying points for educated blacks and served as the forum for political discussions and exchange of views. They also formed the backbone of the growth of black financial institutions later on.

In addition, some of the societies maintained strong magazines to inform and influence public opinion: the Phi Beta Sigma Fraternity and *The Crescent,* the Alpha Phi Alpha Fraternity and the *Sphinx,* and the Independent Order of St. Luke and the *Herald.* They were also avenues of racial solidarity and the development of black entrepreneurship in education and business. While they have been attacked for irrelevancies recently, they have clearly served a significant function, although sometimes obscured by superficialities, in maintaining a degree of social cohesion within our community.

EMIGRATION IDEAS

Disappointment with the socio-economic difficulties in the American society forced some blacks as early as the mid-nineteenth century to advocate emigration to a location, where, they believed, they would have the best opportunities for developing themselves and for improving their condition. Unlike Garvey's movement of a later period, their's was comprised of largely elite organizations, led by successful businessmen who had been in the vanguard of the fight for equal rights within the nation but, having been frustrated, saw Africa or other areas outside the United States as the final alternative.

S. Wesley Jones of Tuscaloosa, Alabama, petitioned the American Colonization Society in June 1848 for funds to sail to Liberia and to establish business there. The colonization spirit that grew in Alabama at this time was not limited to this state but was evident in other states as well. Though Jones did not get the free "passage and six months' support" he asked for, he remained a great advocate of emigration to the end. In a resolution by the Movement Among the Colored People of Cincinnati, Ohio (July 1850), the blacks of this city urged colonization in Liberia since continued stay in America would never yield social or political equality.

In 1954, Martin R. Delaney, and others in a lengthy memorandum entitled *Political Destiny of the Colored Race on the American Continent,* strongly proposed emigration. They argued that to continue to be "sparsely interspersed among our white fellow-countrymen, we never might be expected to equal them in any branch or respectable competition for a livelihood." The group advocated emigration not to Africa but to Central, South America, the West Indies, or to West Canada under proper safeguards.

The same feelings of territorial separation and emigration were echoed in the 1870s, this time among the masses of Mound Bayou, Mississippi. Even Church leaders like Bishop Henry M. Turner were prominent in the agitation. As economic conditions worsened and racism grew, interest in the possibilities of migrating to a suitable location became more insistent. In 1876 leaders of the Kansas exodus testified to the Select Committee of the United States Senate and requested removal of blacks from the southern states to the northern states. In 1877, a group of interested blacks in South Carolina petitioned the President of Liberia asking to go to that country and settle. While the signatories and the more than 150,000 blacks they represented were in the planning stage, a Norfleet Browne was reporting of his favorable reception in Liberia in 1880.

To Bishop Henry M. Turner again, however, white America should pay an indemnity of $40 million to enable black people to go to Africa. At the same time (1900) he denounced those of his race who preferred to migrate to the West rather than go to Africa. Echoing the indemnity slogan once more was Arthur A. Anderson, who in 1913, on behalf of the Colored Liberty League, prepared an Indemnity and Land Bill for Congress. These, of course, were the precursors of Garvey's movement in the 1920s, which, as we have seen already, was a compelling force in American life. In the present decade we hear through the Nation of Islam the old plea for a separation of the races. Elijah Muhammad and his adherents pleaded for funds to develop a separate state inside the United States. Such a state was to have numerous resources and be financially supported for upwards of twenty-five years until it became self-supporting.

We see in the above cases attempts to solve the deteriorating conditions of blacks by separation. History furnishes numerous examples of such movements—the Jewish exodus to Egypt and the English pilgrims and their settlement on the American soil. What is peculiar in our case is the deprivation of the wealth needed to carry on a successful emigration. Dependence on Congress or a philanthropic organization to move some ten million people was in itself frightening for those financing it. Thus blacks have continued to maintain the uneasy equilibrium in the American society, attempting to accommodate to it while resenting its unwholesome aspects.

SOME FORMS OF ECONOMIC NATIONALISM

The methods of effecting economic changes in the black community are various, ranging from the insurrections of slavery times to the learning of skills for meaningful employment and the more radical forms like propaganda and boycotts. A brief history of the latter will demonstrate the efforts of blacks to patronize their own businesses and to instill habits of industry among themselves. These efforts to support black business ranked in importance with the emphasis on race solidarity and race pride, the dominant doctrines of radical blacks throughout the last century.

One or the earliest known conventions for the support of black business took place in Kansas City in 1879. This convention established, among others, two committees on farming and mercantile industries. The first committee recommended that members should regard farming as an honorable and lucrative business and as a sure road to individual independence. It also recommended the holding of fairs in Leavenworth, Kansas, to popularize the work of farmers, mechanics, and artisans in the states of Colorado, Iowa, Nebraska, Missouri, and Kansas.

The mercantile industries committee of this Kansas City convention, which was given the responsibility of securing a better representation for colored men in the mercantile industries of the country, encouraged its members to engage in individual enterprises of a mercantile nature, to set up places of business, and to establish cooperative stores and joint stock companies for lumbering, milling, wood and coal yards, mining, fishing, and similar occupations. The committee also encouraged the patronage of black enterprises and the purchase of their products. Above all, it insisted upon proper preparation for vocations, the amassing of necessary capital, provision of the quality and quantity of products in demand by the community, and the sale of these at competitive prices.

From the above history, we observe how black conventions were speeding the development of black business by advocating cooperative action. The same spirit is echoed in a report of the fifth annual convention of the National Negro Business League, 1904, in Pensacola, Florida. Here a Mr. Fred R. Moore insisted that the way to organize was to get all individuals interested in the advancement of the race and of their communities together, so that they could pledge themselves to the support of enterprises managed by men and women of the race. Members, he said, should patronize the black drug store, medical doctor, and lawyer. In addition, they were enjoined to subscribe to literature published by members of the black race.

Mr. Moore suggested that local leagues should serve as chambers of commerce for the race, to guard and protect the people against unwise investments, to expose fake companies, to suggest improvements, insist on fair business practices, and, above all, to control the employment of labor among the line advocated for black economic development. Such cooperatives received a great stimulus from the writings of W. E. B. Du Bois, who by 1917 was using the pages of the *Crisis* to propagate his ideas on the subject. Progress in cooperatives was evident in many parts of the country. By 1919 the Citizens' Cooperative Stores opened a unit in Memphis, Tennessee, under the leadership of Mr. B. M. Roddy, who himself was influenced by Du Bois. This store, though capitalized at $5,000, was oversubscribed within a month. The charter was thenceforth amended and capitalized at $15,000. Within four months there were five similar stores opened to serve the needs of black buyers and sellers in Memphis.

One of the foremost boycott organizations among blacks was the New Negro Alliance, incorporated in Washington, D.C. This organization began in the throes of the American Depression, and its strong emphasis was on combating employment discrimination by obtaining jobs for black workers in white-owned businesses in the ghetto. The organization utilized the strategies of picketing to force business to meet its demands. As a pressure group it was successful in a variety of cases in organizing black consumers and getting them to support or withhold their support from designated stores and other business enterprises, making the latter employ blacks in good numbers. Other organizations sharing the black business philosophy were the League for Fair Play and the Afro-American Federation Blacks. In essence, there was a prevailing philosophy among blacks that if success came it would be by blacks working together.

Mr. F. J. Weaver was one of the leaders of the Business League in Kansas City, Missouri. In 1913 he was urging blacks of all classes and professions to "support the negro in business and help our race to get on its feet in your community." In this city, he reported that most blacks were already making progress economically because they supported one another, and that Kansas City, Missouri, was already known as the "town of home-buyers among negroes."

By the turn of the present century the idea of patronizing black business had gained momentum. Slogans like "double-duty-dollar" and "buy black" were becoming current. Their aim was to safeguard black businesses and to provide attendant advantages. In 1915 an editorial in the *Sunshine,* a newspaper published in Oakland, California, strongly suggested the widespread formation of Negro Business Leagues. The writer enumerated their advantages and the steps by which such formation could be accomplished. The league was to encompass, as far as possible, every facet of economic life. Preachers had a special and vital role in spreading the gospel of wealth from the pulpit. Patronage of black business was seen by the newspaper as the sure economic foundation for the present and future of the black race.

The development of cooperation among blacks was long a significant step in fighting racism. Many organizations, like the New Negro Alliance, employed the economic weapons of boycott and picketing under the racial symbols of "Don't Buy Where You Can't Work," or "Buy Where You Can Work." The objectives of the organizations were definitely not exclusively economic. Some were political, racial, or cultural; but the economic factor still remained dominant. The economic boycotts have aimed at persuading white business to adopt employment and other measures favorable to urban and rural ghetto inhabitants. One of the most recent economic boycotts organized by blacks to increase their participation in the American economy was "Operation Breadbasket," the brainchild of Dr. Martin Luther King and the economic arm of the Southern Christian Leadership Conference. It was later led by Jesse Jackson who split with SCLC over strategies for the organization and subsequently created Operation PUSH. Operation PUSH, like Breadbasket, uses a fourfold strategy—selective buying, securing of employment, boycotting, and picketing—to obtain benefits and better conditions of service for blacks.

The National Urban League

The problems of unemployment and adjustment to the northern industrial society for migrant blacks from the agricultural South after the Civil War were great and far-reaching. The most important organization that emerged to tackle these problems was the National Urban League, estabilshed in 1911. It was the brain work of Booker T. Washington and a group of black and white philanthropists, largely businessmen, professionals, and like-minded people interested in the economic and social rehabilitation of migrant blacks. These individuals were mostly interested in social work and self-help—more than in militancy or protest. The league's attachment to Booker T. Washington and the Tuskegee Institute in Alabama is evidence enough of the latter's influence on the philosophy and mode of operations of the former.

Washington believed that discrimination of all sorts, in industry and elsewhere, was the result of the lack of skill and the careless habits of the black worker. To remove this problem, he proposed an increase in employment for blacks and an improvement of the quality of black labor. In turn the National Urban League accepted his philosophy and stressed self-improvement, the virtues of skill, hard work, and thrift among black workers. Owing to the many obstacles facing them—lynchings, race riots, disfranchisement, Jim Crow Laws, peonage on cotton plantations, and the discriminatory practices of the American Federation of Labor—the league adopted diplomatic approaches in dealing with white employers. However, its methods were interpreted by the blacks of radical persuasion and their sympathizers as "selling" black people's labor to white employers.

In spite of this criticism, the National Urban League insisted on creating an understanding between black workers and white employers, even giving the whites a voice in the management of its affairs. Its conciliatory attitude was also a means of obtaining the necessary financial support from prominent white industrialists and philanthropists. From its inception the league operated an employment agency and created associations of black workers in order to train them efficiently in the various vocations in which they had to perform. The league's attempts to move blacks into skilled jobs were, however, frustrated by the poor economic conditions of the times.

The improvement of the quality of black labor was another preoccupation of the league. To do this, its New York local branch formed organizations of mechanics, elevator men, bellmen, pullman porters, and chauffeurs. It achieved great successes during World War I, when it placed a large number of employees in war industries. Since the midle 1920s, the league has instituted an annual "Negro Industrial Week," through the expanding local branches, to advertise black people's labor to white businesses and employers.

In the 1930s the league initiated the annual "Negro Vocational Opportunity Campaign" aimed at encouraging high school and college youth to prepare themselves for better grades of employment. The league's industrial department, on the other hand, shifted its activity to vocational guidance and held occasional conferences to teach blacks to be good workers. It increased its activity in referring blacks throughout the country for job openings in industry and in the fields of domestic and menial labor.

The National Urban League, as a result of its interracial policy, sometimes ran into difficulties with employers of labor. Though it had courted their favor and profited from their financial support, the league found their attitude to black labor unacceptable. Since black labor was regarded by whites as a competitor in the labor market, organized white labor in collusion with employers tried to keep blacks out of skilled jobs. The league attempted, in 1920 and in 1925, in cooperation with the NAACP and AFL, to solve these problems—but to no avail. Failing in this, the league was forced to acquiesce and to align itself with the employers.

Another area of conflict was in colective bargaining. In 1919 the National Urban League passed resolutions endorsing the principle of collective bargaining for black workers. It discouraged the use of blacks as strike-breakers but favored their entering into trade unions and their organizing with whites only when conditions were favorable, while providing the alternative that, if this tactic failed, blacks should organize themselves to bargain with employers and organized labor. Owing to its belief in the advantages of organized labor, as against strike-breaking, the league, in cooperation with the New York Labor Movement, established in 1925 the short-lived Trade Unions Committee for Organized Black Workers.

Local leagues were, however, not enamored of the policies of the parent body, especially with regard to strike breaking. Supported by local businessmen who were convinced that organized labor could not be trusted and that after a successful strike the blacks would be eliminated by the union, the local Chicago league, between 1920 and 1930, deliberately supplied strike-breakers to employers. It was further argued that the gains in job status won by blacks during strikes were rarely maintained after they were over. As a result the local leagues tended to aid antiunion employers. This was, and remains, a dilemma for the National Urban League. In the context of the vicissitudes of the American labor market, it was hard to find a middle way.

During the depression years of 1930 and 1940 the National Urban League made desperate efforts to create employment and equal opportunity for black workers and to condemn gross exploitation in the War Department's Mississippi River flood control project and the exclusion of black workers from the construction of Boulder Dam. The league also succeeded in organizing workers' councils during the mid-1930s in over one hundred cities and in educating black workers in the principles of trade unionism. Significant achievements were made from 1940 to 1945 when defense employment began to rise. During this period the National Urban League and some other civil rights organizations began again to pressure the government to open employment in aircraft, in war industries, and in military installation programs. At the same time the league was able to get blacks into government training programs for war industries and into some of the highly discriminatory building trade unions in several cities.

The change of strategies crept into the open between 1945 and 1960. While maintaining blacks in their minimal employment, the league emphasized their placement in jobs that members of the race had never held before. There was the example of the Pilot Placement Program of 1947, which resulted in a mere token employment of overqualified blacks. Better success was achieved with the Vocational Guidance Program and the cooperation with industrial personnel in instituting college career conferences. By 1949 the league had succeeded in persuading industrial employers to conduct job interviews at a black university for the first time in history. It further established a liaison with labor leaders and consulted with officials of government agencies. Through these intensive activities the league tried to convince businessmen of the advantages of employing blacks.

The change in the strategy of the National Urban League was seen more in the 1960s when it moved from nonviolence to more aggressive policies. Its leaders, emboldened by the militancy of other black organizations, effectively presented arguments to government, industry, and the public in a campaign to eliminate discrimination. Thus the National Urban League was the first civil rights organization to introduce the idea of compensatory employment policies, later adopted by other more radical civil rights groups.

In 1963 Whitney Young, the league's past president, introduced what he styled the "Domestic Marshall Plan" to help unemployed deprived blacks overcome their disabilities resulting from three centuries of deprivation. The plan advocated special treatment for black people to prepare them to compete with others on a level of equality. It was not enough to decree equality by law, the plan insisted. Genuine equality must begin when blacks have equal training and skills to utilize the new opportunities. The plan therefore emphasized manpower training, youth motivation, and general education. In addition, it recommended family strengthening to bring deprived blacks to the point where they would not be at a disadvantage in competition.

The league's aggressive attitude produced baffling results. For the first time since its inception, it found itself by 1964 unable to meet the demands of white employers for black workers. The situation was also created by the type of relationship between white employers and the league as opposed to that of the NAACP, CORE, and other militant groups. As the pressure from black power advocates increased, more and more white employers increasingly turned to local urban leagues for help in obtaining black labor. Because the league could not meet this demand adequately, it created a "Skills Bank," a roster of people with skills needed by industry whose training could not be used in the past because of white employers' racism.

The achievements of the Urban League cannot be measured in statistics alone, as much of its work is public relations and social welfare. However, a few figures give an idea of the work already accomplished. In 1968 the league affiliates secured 50,000 new jobs through contracts with local businessmen. The 18,085 individuals who registered in the league's National Skills Bank were upgraded to better jobs. This figure included 2,331 in professional categories and 800 in sales jobs. From 1964 it negotiated contracts that provided on-the-job training for 2,600 individuals. Of these 87 percent were "hard-core" jobless. As a result of the contract by the league, 89.4 percent of the trainees got permanent jobs.

Another program of the league is "Operation Equality," to be discussed below, which aims at creating a climate in the cities and suburbs in which residents will be acceptable to the public. The program also persuades high school dropouts to resume their education. By 1969 the league had 93 local affiliates, 1,600 employees and a biracial board of trustees that included some of the most prominent men in American business.

The National Urban Leaue has emerged from the position of petitioner for black employment to that of spokesman. Its influence in pressuring businesses to accept its recommendations reached a high point under Whitney Young. Although it does not normally participate in direct-action demonstrations, it has begun to utilize some of the strategies of the more militant civil rights organizations. Through careful negotiations and the avoidance of direct action, however, the National Urban League retains the confidence of businessmen and interprets to them the aspirations of the black worker.

THE NATION OF ISLAM: A FRATERNAL SOCIETY

Athough the preoccupation of the Nation of Islam was initially religious, nevertheless the organization has ventured into social and economic activities, and it is in this light that we shall now discuss it.

Utilizing the unifying symbols of race and religion, the late Elijah Muhammad, the founder of the Nation of Islam, the foremost mass Black Nationalist movement of the second half of the century, set out certain incentives to attack the ills besetting blacks in the American society. Chief among these is the belief that they are laying the foundation for a Black Nation. Second, they believe that in Islam, and particularly in the Nation of Islam, they can enjoy freedom, fraternity, justice, and equality under their own government, which the American myth has denied them. Third, they believe that their lives will be morally and materially improved once they have accepted Islam as a way of life.

While the National Association for the Advancement of Colored People and the National Urban League are largely middle and upper-class movements of blacks and whites, the Black Muslims is by contrast a mass movement, catering to the interests of hundreds of thousands of lower class blacks all over the nation and serving as an inspiration to other black movements.

The need for group identity and the desire for self-improvement are the two principal motives that lead individuals to join and to remain in the Nation of Islam.

The Nation of Islam stresses the importance of economic self-sufficiency as an instrument of racial advancement and asserts that the black man is responsible for his own economic advancement. Among the Muslims, hard work, thrift, and accumulation of wealth have a religiouslike sanction, hence the following "Economic Blue Print for the Black Man" by the organization:

1. That blacks recognize the necessity for unity and group activities.
2. To pool their resources together.
3. To stop disparaging everything that is black-owned and black-operated.

The organization of the economic activities of a temple is described as "communalism." It is a system in which followers voluntarily and regularly give part of their income toward the establishment of small business enterprises, although they are under no obligation to do so when they cannot afford it. The Nation of Islam's communalism attempts to fulfill three objectives: (1) to inculcate, through thrift, a sense of responsibility for economic self-improvement; (2) to provide a channel for investments created through collective business enterprises owned by the temple; and (3) to develop a sense of responsibility for the welfare of the community.

The followers also expect to profit from their contributions to the nation in time of sickness, unemployment, or old age. Members of the nation claim to be generally economically more secure than many blacks from similar low-income backgrounds. Elimination of expenditures on such nonessential items as tobacco, liquor, gambling, and popular entertainments (all of which are prohibited by the religion) has enabled them to utilize their income more efficiently.

The Nation of Islam advocates black ownership of landed businesses. In this light we can say they are in the vanguard of black capitalism, which they feel is natural and necessary. Black men and women need to be involved in all forms of economic activity that are the inevitable communications between nations and peoples.

They also see agriculture as a major means to black liberation. A few quotes from the progress section of the April 27, 1970, issue of *Muhammad Speaks* illustrates this:

> *We are walking on Bread daily*
> *Bread is in the earth*
> *Money, clothes, homes, and all*
> *the necessities of life are*
> *under our feet!*
>
> *We must do something for ourselves.*
> *Dig into the earth for self*
>
> *Surely the white race has been very good*
> *in the making of jobs for their willing slaves*
> *But this cannot go on forever.*
> *We are about at the end of it and must do*
> *something for self, or else!*

This emphasis on agriculture has been substantiated by a purchase of 1,000 acres of farm and ranch land in St. Clair County, Alabama. It is important to note that St. Clair County is 85 percent white. The Nation of Islam intends to turn the farm into a "showplace" of the South with the major task of providing high quality food for restaurants and markets in several large Northern cities. They plan to eventually turn the ranch into a $25 million processing complex.

The $750,000 farm has its own meatpacking and vegetable canning plant. It will provide 150 needed jobs, add taxes to the county's income, and boost business of local suppliers. There has been strong opposition to the Nation of Islam. They include law suits and open confrontation as they push on their agricultural projects. Yet their courage is not daunted.

The Nation of Islam owns a $125,000 meat processing plant in Chicago, a $500,000 farm and dairy and orchard in Michigan, and a modern restaurant-supermarket complex in Chicago. It is important to note that the Nation of Islam does not hesitate to purchase white expertise or use whites as intermediaries. An excellent manifestation of this is the farm in Alabama sold to Black Muslims by the well-known segregationist Roy Wyatt. He serves as personnel manager of this enterprise, and in return the nation promises to buy trucks and cars from him. This action coincides with the philosophy of Booker T. Washington when he said, "In all things that are purely social we can be as separate as the fingers, yet one as the hand in all things essential to mutual progress." In a real sense Booker T. Washington's views were similar to those of the late Elijah Muhammad. This is evident when Washington expressed his philosophies of racial solidarity and economic nationalism. Both urged the patronage of black businesses.

Furthermore, Washington's philosophy of wealth and property ownership as the basis for respect for blacks permeates Muslim economic thought. Malcolm X once talked about how people used to joke about the "Ching Chong Chinaman." He pointed out that few people do that now, in that China has emerged as a major world power technologically, militarily, and economically. In short the whole world respects China. In an effort to attain this respect the Muslims have worked toward a Muslim-owned financial empire that someday will lead to a separate, self-sufficient "Black Islam Nation" within the continental United States.

In 1968 alone the Muslims sank approximately $6 million in business and real estate. In Chicago's South Side ghetto the organization owns a warehouse, apartment houses, 2 bakeries, a clothing store, 2 restaurants, and 2 supermarkets where produce is sold bearing the Muslim's "Your" label. The Muslims operate a string of stores in Cleveland. In Washington, D.C., they own a bakery, barber shop, restaurant, cleaning establishment, and a printing office.

The Muslims have rehabilitated and equipped a unique headquarters in an abandoned 4-story factory on Chicago's South Side to handle meat processing, garment making, central accounting, and a newspaper that publishes the weekly *Muhammad*

Speaks with over 500,000 copies circulation. The building is equipped with computerized typesetting and 4-color printing presses.

In the past, most funds have come from the Muslims themselves in the form of membership titles, but they now negotiate loans from various banks. Part of this money is used for additional business investment, a third being spent to revitalize the 47 Muslim schools throughout the country and the 37-year-old University of Islam.

The Black Muslims as a socio-economic *cum* religious organization have succeeded in teaching hard work, thrift, and service to the community. Their agricultural and industrial projects demonstrate what can be achieved where there is goodwill, determination, and organizational ability. Espousing economic self-sufficiency and the separation of the races, except for "essential" social contacts, the Black Muslims' aim is to enable the black to attain a certain measure of self-reliance, without which opportunity the blacks would be crowded out by the white economic system.

CONCLUSIONS

1. PRESENT KNOWLEDGE of Afro-American experience in the United States economy is gleaned from literature that is largely racially biased. White and black writers have tended to go to extremes in dealing with the question. For an objective treatment there should be an interdisciplinary approach drawing not only from the arts but also from the social and physical sciences. Popular periodicals and newspapers should be supplemented by learned journals and standard works written by scholars of all races.

2. IN THE MATTER of the African past there is still more work to be done. Physicists, economists, historians, and others should join with anthropologists and sociologists in excavating and interpreting the African heritage and placing it in its proper perspective. They need to be encouraged by the universities, African Studies Centers, Afro-American Studies Centres, and national governments.

3. TO PUT OUR KNOWLEDGE of Afro-American contribution to American agriculture in its proper perspective, the works of the older writers like Phillips and Tillinghast must be matched by those of Conrad, Meyer, Genovese, and Gray. To the historical, descriptive approach must be added new tools of analysis like economic theory and econometrics.

4. AN EQUITABLE PLACE of Afro-Americans in the scheme of things will connote their greater participation in the fruits of

modern industrialization and the gradual but steady extinction of the ghetto with all its deprivation and economic disincentive. The leadership of black intellectuals in business will assure more employment and higher income for their less privileged racial grouping.

5. FUTURE STRATEGIES to enhance an effective black role in the labor market should include increased investment in the human potential, job creation, manpower training, and the elimination of discriminatory practices of labor unions and employment agencies.

It is to be expected that there will come about changes in the place of black women in the labor force as well. Industialization and the realization of the above suggestions will affect the structure and direction of the trend. It can be safely said, however, that the future will see the women sharing the burdens of the family with the men rather than having to carry them all alone.

6. BLACK ENTREPRENEURIAL HISTORY is replete with the knowledge of the blacks who have given thought to the direction in which the race should go, the need to meet the demands of America's growing society and multiplying processes and techniques, and the blacks' inability to catch up with the tempo of development in the white community.

It is the duty of the affected blacks to study in greater depth new ideas on black development and record any success stories that can serve as inspiration to many. The importance of this task is so great that colleges, universities, and foundations should find it a necessary field to support.

7. ON EDUCATION, we have observed the ills of segregation, low standards, defeatism, and the prevalence of slave mentality. American educational institutions can contribute to social harmony by changing these traits and giving the youths the proper orientation. Other enabling strategies are desegregation, proper curriculum, equipment, and a good staff.

8. THE HISTORY of immigration into the United States proves that collective efforts are valuable in meeting certain peculiar needs of groups. As Afro-Americans cannot expect to build a

separate society through emigration, which was the objective of W. E. B. Du Bois, it follows, from the example of other racial groups, that they must find the solutions to their problems themselves here in their own country. Or as Frederick Douglass has aptly put it:

> *We are here,* and here we are likely to be. To imagine that we shall ever be eradicated is absurd and ridiculous. We can be re-modified, changed and assimilated, but never extinguished. We repeat therefore, that *we are here;* and that this is *our* country. . . . We shall neither die out, nor be driven out; but shall go with this people either as a testimony against them, or as an evidence in their favour throughout their generations.

But it is not enough to remain here. Playing the role of full citizens is vital, which means that blacks must achieve those objectives that had previously been sought through the advocation of emigration, the founding of welfare organizations, and the taking up of arms as the last resort. It is necessary to channel the individual aspirations and aims into group or organizational aims and aspirations. Black communities and self-help organizations are invaluable here in giving these a national character for social change, while preserving their peculiar characteristics.

The Rotary Club, Lion's Club, and Kiwanis of the white community as well as their national and church groups are self-help organizations rendering useful services to the society. It is in this context that I see a beneficial role in the similar organizations of blacks. Only in the black cultural group can the people define their roles and maintain their identity. Afro-Americans therefore can hope to attain full citizenship in the American society without sacrificing racial identity.

The task of building up an economy of a whole nation is a colossal one. Judging by past experience, Afro-Americans have played enviable roles and made great achievements that have defied all expectations. It is only logical therefore to maintain that they will continue the struggle relentlessly, improving on all sides all the time and maintaining a viable existence in this plural society.

NOTES

CHAPTER ONE

1. Eli Hecksher, "A Plea for Theory in Economic History," *Enterprise and Secular Change,* III (1953): 423. *See also* John Clapham, "Survey of Development to the Twentieth Century," *Encyclopedia of the Social Sciences* (1931): 327 f.; Ernest Nagel, "Some Issues in the Logic of Historical Analysis," *Scientific Monthly,* 74: 163 f.
2. Ralph Andreano, "Four Recent Studies in American Economic History," *New Views on American Economic Development,* ed. R. L. Andreano (Cambridge, Massachusetts: Schenkman Publishing Company, 1965), p. 28 f.; Fritz Redlich, "New and Traditional Approaches to Economic History," *Journal of Economic History,* XXV (December, 1965): 482.
3. Carter Goodrich, "Economic History: One Field or Two," *Readings in United States Economic and Business History,* ed. Ross M. Robertson and James L. Pate (New York: Houghton Mifflin Company, 1966), p. 23.
4. Thomas E. Leslie, "On the Philosophical Method of Political Economy," *Readings in United States Economic and Business History,* p. 7 f.; Redlich, "New and Traditional Approaches to Economic History and Their Interdependence," pp. 480-95.
5. Lance E. Davis, Jonathan Hughes, and Stanley Reiter, "Aspects of Quantitative Research in Economic History," *Journal of Economic History,* XX (December, 1960): 539-47; Doug-

lass North, "Quantitative Research in American History," *American Economic Review,* LIII (March, 1963): 125-30; John R. Meyer and Alfred H. Conrad, "Economic Theory, Statistical Inference, and Economic History," *Journal of Economic History,* XVII: 524-44.

6. Edwin R. A. Seligman, *The Economic Interpretation of History* (New York: Columbia University Press, 1962), p. 3. For views on Black History, *see* Melvin Drimmer, *Black History: A Reappraisal* (New York: Doubleday & Company, 1968); Dwight W. Hoover, *Understanding Negro History* (Chicago: Quadrangle Books, 1968); A. A. Taylor, "Historians of the Reconstruction," *Journal of Negro History,* XXIII (January, 1938).

7. W. W. Rostow, *The Stages of Economic Growth* (New York: Cambridge University Press, 1960).

8. Leif Johansen, *A Multi-Sectoral Study of Economic Growth* (Amsterdam: 1960), p. 8.

9. Colin Clark, *Conditions of Economic Progress,* 3rd ed. (London: Macmillan, 1957); also Richard T. Gill, *Economic Development: Past and Present* (Englewood Cliffs, New Jersey: Prentice-Hall, 1964), pp. 22-23.

10. Karl Marx and Friedrich Engels, *The Communist Manifesto,* 1940; Karl Marx, *Capital* (Chicago: Charles H. Kerr & Company, 1908). For further approaches to the study of economic growth and economic history *see* L. E. Ayres, *The Theory of Economic Progress* (New York: Schocken Books, 1962); Fried. Bearwald, *History and Structure of Economic Development* (Scranton, Pennsylvania: International Textbook Company, 1969); John Clapham, "Survey of Development to the Twentieth Century."

11. Harold D. Woodman, *Slavery and the Southern Economy* (San Francisco: Harcourt Brace World, 1966), p. 247.

CHAPTER TWO

1. Henry Highland Garnet, "The Past and the Present Condition, and the Destiny of the Colored Race" (Discourse

delivered at the Fiftieth Anniversary of the Female Benevolent Society of Troy, New York, February 14, 1848), J. C. Kneeland & Company, 1848, pp. 6-12.

2. Arthur A. Schomburg, "Racial Integrity: A Plea for the Establishment of a Chair of Negro History in Our Schools and Colleges," *Negro Society for Historical Research, Occasional Papers,* no. 3 (1913): 17-19.

3. Carter G. Woodson, *The Association for the Study of Negro Life and History,* leaflet, 1947, quoted by J. H. Bracey, Jr.; August Meier and E. Rudwick, *Black Nationalism in America* (Indianapolis, Indiana: The Bobbs-Merrill Company, 1970), p. 317.

4. Monroe N. Work, "The Passing Tradition and the African Civilization," *Journal of Negro History,* I (January, 1916): 34-41.

5. Herodotus, *The History of Herodotus,* ed. Komroff (New York: Tudor Publishing Company, 1956); Leo Africanus, *The History and Description of Africa,* vol. I, ed. Robert Brown (New York: B. Franklin, 1963); Eudre Sik, *The History of Black Africa,* vol. I (Budapest: Akademiai Kiado, 1966); Henry Cary, *The Histories of Herodotus* (New York: D. Appleton Publishers, 1904); Ricky Rosenthal, *The Splendor That Was Africa* (Dobbs Ferry, New York: Ocean Publications, 1967).

6. George P. Murdock, *Africa: Its Peoples and Their Cultural History* (New York: 1959), pp. 40-45 and 64-67; Christopher Wrigley, "Speculation on the Economic Pre-History of Africa," *Journal of African History,* I, no. 2: 189-203; J. D. Fage, "Anthropology, Botany, and the History of Africa," *Journal of African History,* II, no. 2 (1902): 302-4; M. J. Herskovits, *The Human Factor in Changing Africa* (New York: Alfred A. Knopf, 1962), p. 51 f.; Paul Bohannan, "The Agricultural Revolution," *Africa and the Africans* (Garden City, New York: The Natural History Press, 1964), pp. 80-85.

7. Basil Davidson, *The African Past* (Boston: Little, Brown and Company, 1964), p. 67.

CHAPTER THREE

1. Cf. Willie J. King, *The Negro in American Life* (New York: 1926), p. 50.

2. Benjamin Brawley, *A Social History of the American Negro* (New York: 1921), p. 8.

3. W. E. B. Du Bois, *The Negro* (New York: Henry Holt and Company), p. 155.

4. Cf. K. O. Dike, *Trade and Politics in the Niger Delta* (New York: Oxford University Press, 1956). The number suggested here is 6 million.

5. William A. Sinclair, *The Aftermath of Slavery* (Boston: 1905), p. 9.

6. Robert C. Weaver, *Negro Labor—A National Problem* (New York: 1946), p. 3.

7. Attempts at measuring the economic factors of slavery are recent. A few can be mentioned: Alfred H. Conrad and John R. Meyer, *The Economics of Slavery* (Chicago: 1964); Louis A. Rose, "Capital Losses of Southern Share-Holders Due to Emancipation," *Western Economic Journal*, III (Fall, 1964); U. B. Phillips, "The Economic Cost of Slaveholding in the Cotton Belt," *Political Science Quarterly*, XX (1905): 257-75; T. F. Kettel, *Southern Wealth and Northern Profits* (New York: 1860), p. 48; Kenneth M. Stampp, *The Peculiar Institution* (New York: 1956); Eugene D. Genovese, *The Political Economy of Slavery* (New York: Random House, 1965), pp. 62-179.

For the methodology of computing productivity and profitability of antebellum slave labor, *see* the excellent studies by James D. Foust and Dale E. Swan, "Productivity and Profitability of Antebellum Slave Labour: A Micro-Approach," *Agricultural History*, XLIX, no. 1 (January, 1970): 39-62; Alfred H. Conrad and John R. Meyer, "The Economics of Slavery in the Antebellum South," *Journal of Political Economy*, 66 (April, 1964): 325-32; Richard Sutch, "The Profitability of Antebellum Slavery—Revised," *Southern Economic Journal*, 31 (April, 1965): 365-83; Robert R.

Russell, "The Effects of Slavery upon Non-Slaveholders in the Antebellum South," *Agricultural History,* XII (April, 1941): 112-26, reprinted in Harold P. Woodman, *Slavery and the Southern Economy* (New York: Harcourt Brace World, 1966); Robert W. Fogel and Stanley L. Engerman, "The Economics of Slavery," *The Reinterpretation of American Economic History* (New York: Harper & Row, Publishers); Alfred H. Conrad et al., "Slavery as an Obstacle to Economic Growth in the United States," *Journal of Economic History,* XXVII (December, 1967): 518-60; William N. Parker, "Slavery and Southern Economic Development: An Hypothesis and Some Evidence," *Agricultural History,* XLIX, no. 1 (January, 1970): 115-25.

8. J. Tillinghast, *The Negro in Africa and America* (New York: Macmillan, 1902), p. 137.

9. Adam Smith, *Wealth of Nations,* quoted by U. B. Phillips, *American Negro Slavery* (New York: 1918), p. 347.

10. Weaver, p. 4.

11. C. M. Melden, *From Slave to Citizen* (1921), p. 203.

12. Kenneth M. Stampp, "Negro Poverty under Slavery," *Poverty—American Style,* ed. H. P. Miller (California: 1966), p. 20.

13. C. Silberman, *Crisis in Black and White* (New York: Vintage Books, 1964), p. 253; W. Galenson and C. Pyatt, *The Quality of Labor* (Geneva: ILO, 1964); T. W. Shultz, "Investment in Human Capital," *American Economic Review* (March, 1961); T. W. Schultz, *The Economic Value of Education* (New York: Columbia University Press, 1963).

14. L. Gray, *History of Agriculture in Southern United States to 1860* (New York: Macmillan, 1902).

15. Phillips, "The Economic Cost of Slaveholding in the Cotton Belt," p. 137.

16. Meyer Jacobstein, *Tobacco Industry in the United States* (1907).

17. E. N. Elliott, *Cotton Is King,* quoted by Willie J. King, *The Negro in American Life,* pp. 52-53. The higher return on female labor was based on the expectation of its productivity in births.

18. C. M. Melden, *From Slave to Citizen* (1921), p. 200, quoted by King, p. 51.
19. Elliott, p. 55, quoted by King, p. 52.
20. David L. Cohn, *The Life and Times of King Cotton* (New York: Oxford University Press, 1966), p. 16.
21. U. F. Faulkner, *American Economic History* (New York: Harper & Row, Publishers, 1960), p. 201.
22. Woodman, *Slavery and the Southern Economy*, p. 192.
23. T. Dew, quoted by Faulkner, p. 316.
24. Woodman, p. 201.

CHAPTER FOUR

1. Avery Odell Graven, "Soil Exhaustion as a Factor in the Agricultural History of Virginia and Maryland, 1606-1860," *University of Illinois Studies in the Social Sciences* (Urbana, Illinois: University of Illinois, 1926), p. 24.
2. Eugene D. Genovese, *The Political Economy of Slavery* (New York: Random House, 1965), p. 110.
3. C. K. Meek, *Land, Law and Customs in the Colonies* (New York: Oxford University Press, 1949), p. 197.
4. S. F. Nadel, *A Black Byzantium, The Kingdom of Nupe in Nigeria* (New York: Oxford University Press, 1951), p. 105.
5. Genovese, p. 77; also Nadel, p. 358.
6. Meek, p. 153.
7. Sir Alan Burns, *History of Nigeria* (London: George Allen and University, 1963), pp. 151-56.
8. John Hope Franklin, *Reconstruction: After the Civil War* (Chicago: 1961), p. 15; Gilbert H. Barnes, *The Antislavery Impulse* (New York: 1963), p. 53.
9. John S. Ezell, *The South since 1865* (New York: Henry Holt & Company), p. 117.
10. Claude H. Nolen, *The Negro's Image in the South* (Lexington, Kentucky: University of Kentucky Press, 1967), p. 155.
11. Benjamin Brawley, *A Social History of the American Negro* (New York: Macmillan, 1921), p. 292.

12. Edwing R. Embree, *American Negroes: A Handbook* (New York: The John Day Company, 1942), pp. 40-41.
13. Florida State University, *The Negro in American Society* (Tampa, Florida: Florida Grower Press, 1958), p. 40.
14. Victor Perlo, *The Negro in Southern Agriculture* (New York: International Publishers Company, 1953), p. 23; James G. Maddox, *The Advancing South: Manpower Prospects and Problems* (Rahway, New Jersey: Quinn and Boden Company, 1967), pp. 20-21; Anson Phelps-Stokes, *Progress in Negro Status and Race Relations 1911-1946: The Thirty-five Year Report of the Phelps-Stokes Fund* (New York: The Phelps-Stokes Fund, 1948).

CHAPTER FIVE

1. Relevant literature for the Introduction can be found in the following: A. Bonne, *Studies in Economic Development* (London: 1957); C. Clark, *The Conditions of Economic Progress* (London: 1951); W. W. Rostow, *The Stages of Economic Growth* (Cambridge: 1960); R. Nurkse, *Some Aspects of Capital Formation in Underdeveloped Countries* (London: Oxford University Press, 1952); A. Myrdal, *Economic Theory and Underdeveloped Regions* (London: 1957); W. A. Lewis, *Aspects of Industrialization* (1953); United Nations, *Indusetrialization and Productivity Bulletin* 1 (New York: 1958).
2. Of the numerous publications on the black in industry, only a few of the most common will be mentioned here: Walter L. Fleming, *The Freedmen's Savings Bank, A Chapter in the History of the Negro Race* (Chapel Hill, North Carolina: The University of North Carolina Press, 1927); Joseph A. Pierce, *Negro Business Education* (New York: Harper & Row, Publishers, 1947), p. vii; E. Franklin Frazier, *Black Bourgeoisie* (New York: Collier-Macmillan, 1968), p. 55; U.S. Department of Commerce, *Savings and Loan Associations Owned and Operated by Negroes* (Washington, D.C.:

1951); Vishu V. Oak, *The Negro's Adventure in General Business* (Yellow Springs, Ohio: The Antioch Press, 1949), pp. 48-49; Eli Ginzberg, ed., *The Negro Challenge to the Business Community* (New York: McGraw-Hill, 1964); T. L. Cross, *Black Capitalism* (New York: Atheneum, 1969); A. L. Harris, *The Negro as Capitalist* (Philadelphia: 1936); American Assembly, *Black Economic Development* (Englewood Cliffs, New Jersey: Prentice-Hall, 1969); J. H. Harmon, *Negro as Businessman* (1929; reprint ed., College Park, Maryland: McGrath Publishing Company, 1969).

3. Benjamin Brawley, *A Short History of the American Negro* (New York: Macmillan, 1927).

4. A. L. Harris, *The Negro as Capitalist.*

5. Useful books on this section are as follows: A. L. DeMond, *Certain Aspects of the Economic Development of the American Negro, 1865-1900* (Washington, D.C.: Catholic University of America Press, 1945); Robert Kinzer, *The Negro in American Business* (New York: Greenberg, 1950); "The Economics of Liberation," *Ebony* (May, 1969): 150-54; W. F. Haddad, *Black Economic Development* (Englewood Cliffs, New Jersey: Prentice-Hall, 1969); R. P. Derven, "Black Capitalism," *Merchandizing Week* (October 7, 1968); William F. Buckley, Jr., "On Black Capitalism," *National Review* (March 25, 1969); "Symposium on Black Capitalism," *Bankers' Magazine* (Spring, 1969).

6. Langston Hughes, *Famous American Negroes* (New York: Dodd, Mead & Company, 1954), p. 107.

CHAPTER SIX

1. The following are the main sources of reference: Otto Eckstein, *Education, Employment and Negro Equality* (Washington, D.C.: U.S. Department of Labor, 1968); Eugene P. Foley, *The Achieving Ghetto* (Washington, D.C.: The National Press, 1968); *Report of the National Advisory Commission on Civil Disorders* (New York: Bantam Books, 1968); U.S. Bureau of the Census, *The Statistical Abstract of the U.S.* (New York: Grosset and Dunlap, 1969); U.S.

Department of Labor, *Social and Economic Conditions of Negroes in the United States* (Washington, D.C.: U.S. Government Printing Office, 1967).

2. U.S. Department of Commerce, Bureau of the Census, *Current Population Reports,* nos. 135 and 142 (March, 1964); U.S. Department of Commerce, Bureau of the Census, *Current Population Reports* (unpublished data, 1966); U.S. Department of Labor, *Negro Women* (Washington, D.C.: Wage and Labor Standards Administration, 1967); U.S. Department of Labor, *Negro Women in the Population and in the Labor Force* (Washington, D.C.: Wage and Labor Standards Administration).

3. A. B. Jackson, "A Criticism of the Negro Professional," *Journal of Negro History,* ed. Carter G. Woodson (January, 1933): 47-48. Cf. Franklin G. Edwards, *The Negro Professional Class* (Glencoe, Illinois: The Free Press, 1959), p. 24.

4. *Ibid.*

5. Horace Mann Bond, "The Negro Scholar and Professional in America," *The American Negro Reference Book,* vol. 2, ed. John P. Davis (New York: American Book-Stratford Press, 1966), p. 553; Carter G. Woodson, *The Negro Professional Man and the Community* (Washington, D.C.: The Association for the Study of Negro Life and History, 1934), p. 7; Carter G. Woodson, *Negro Makers of History* (Washington, D.C.: The Associated Publishers, 1938).

6. Arnold Rose, *The Negro in America* (New York: Harper and Brothers, 1948), p. 112.

7. Rose, p. 112.

8. For a useful insight into labor-management problems *see:* Thomas O'Hanlon, "The Case against the Unions," *The Negroes and the City* (New York: Time-Life Books, 1968); Herbert Northrup, *Organized Labor and the Negro* (New York: Harper and Brothers, 1964); J. Ray Marshall, *The Negro and Organized Labor* (New York: John Wiley & Sons, 1965); W. E. B. Du Bois, ed. *The College-Bred Negro* (Atlanta: Atlanta University Press, 1900); H. James, A. Borsard, and J. Frederic Duohurst, *University Education for Business* (Philadelphia: University of Pennsylvania Press,

1931) ; The *M.B.A.*, vol. III (April, 1969); Stokeley Carmichael and Charles V. Hamilton, *Black Power* (New York: Random House, 1965); Julius Jacobson, *The Negro and the Labor Movement* (New York: Doubleday & Company, 1968).

9. Rose, *The Negro in America.*

10. A. B. Jackson, "A Criticism of the Negro Professional."

CHAPTER SEVEN

1. Excellent discussions of the functions of the entrepreneur will be found in Arthur H. Cole, "Entrepreneurship and Entrepreneurial History," J. T. Lambie and R. V. Clemence, eds., *Economic Change in America* (Harrisburg, Pennsylvania: 1954), pp. 18-33; Yas wzo Horie, "Modern Entrepreneurship in Meiji Japan," *The State and Economic Enterprise in Japan,* ed. William W. Lockwood (Princeton, New Jersey: Princeton University Press, 1965), pp. 183-208; Joseph Schumpeter, *The Theory of Economic Development* (New York: Oxford University Press, Galaxy edition, 1961), p. 75; Jonathan Hughes, *The Vital Few* (Boston: Houghton Mifflin Company, 1966); L. E. Davis, J. R. T. Hughes, and D. M. McDougall, *American Economic History* (Homewood, Illinois: Richard D. Irwin, 1969); "The Entrepreneurial Factor," *Change and the Entrepreneur,* ed. Arthur Cole (Cambridge, Massachusetts: Harvard University Press, 1949), pp. 7-11; Manley H. Jones, *Executive Decision Making* (Homewood, Illinois: Richard D. Irwin, 1957), pp. 153-71.

2. Articles on the black as entrepreneur can be read in a growing number of journals and books including: Sam A. Levitan, "Entrepreneurship," *Poverty and Human Resources Abstracts* (March-April, 1969): 15-22; Simpson Lawson, "Enterprise," *City* (July-August, 1968): 3-9; Robert B. McKenzie, "Vitalize Black Enterprise," *Harvard Business Review* (September-October, 1968): 88-99; R. C. Puth, "Supreme Life: The History of a Negro Life Insurance Company 1919-1962," *Business History Review* (Spring, 1969): 1-20.

3. Merle Curti, *The Social Ideas of American Educators* (New York: 1935); Gunnar Myrdal, *An American Dilemma,* vol. II (New York: 1944), pp. 897-98; Francis L. Broderick, *W. E. B. Du Bois, Negro Leader in a Time of Crisis* (Stanford, California: Stanford University Press, 1967); Elliott M. Rudwick, *W. E. B. Du Bois, A Study in Minority Group Leadership* (Philadelphia: University of Pennsylvania Press, 1960). *Also see* the following works by W. E. B. Du Bois: *The Souls of Black Folk: Essays and Sketches* (Chicago: 1903); *Dusk of Dawn, An Essay toward the Autobiography of a Race Concept* (New York: 1940); *The Negro in Business* (Boston and Atlanta: 1899); *Black Reconstruction* (New York: Harcourt Brace and Company, 1955); *Efforts for Social Betterment among Negro Americans* (Atlanta, Georgia: Atlanta University Press, 1907); W. E. B. Du Bois, ed., *Economic Cooperation among Negro Americans* (Atlanta, Georgia: Atlanta University Press, 1907).

4. E. David Washington, ed., *Selected Speeches of Booker T. Washington* (Garden City, New York: 1932); Emmett J. Scott and Lyman B. Stowe, *Booker T. Washington: Builder of a Civilization* (Garden City, New York: 1916); Charles S. Johnson, "The Social Philosophy of Booker T. Washington," *Opportunity,* VI (April, 1928); W. Edward Favuson, "Booker T. Washington, A Study in Educational Leadership," *South Atlantic Quarterly,* XLI (July, 1942). *Also see* the following works by Booker T. Washington: *Up from Slavery: An Autobiography* (1900; reprint ed., Williamstown, Massachusetts: Corner House Publishers, 1971); *The Case of the Negro* (Tuskegee, Alabama: 1902); *Sowing and Reaping* (Boston: 1900); "The Best Free Labor in the World," *Southern State Farm Magazine* (January, 1898); "The Negro and the Labor Unions," *Atlantic Monthly,* CXI (June, 1913); "Taking Advantage of Our Disadvantages," *A. M. E. Review,* XX (April, 1894); Booker T. Washington with W. E. B. Du Bois, *The Negro in the South: His Economic Progress in Relation to His Moral and Religious Development* (Philadelphia: 1907); Booker T. Washington and W. E. B. Du

Bois, *The Negro Problem* (New York: James Pott and Company, 1903), pp. 12-13.

5. Malcolm X, *The Autobiography of Malcolm X* (New York: Grove Press, 1965); Louis E. Lomax, *When the Word Is Given: A Report on Elijah Muhammed, Malcolm X and the Black Muslim World* (Cleveland: World Publishing Company, 1963); George Breitman, ed., *Malcolm X Speaks* (New York: Merit Publishers, 1965).

6. Useful study guides include the following: Henry E. Baker, "The Negro in the Field of Invention," *Journal of Negro History*, ed. Carter G. Woodson (January, 1917); Louis Haber, *Black Pioneers of Science and Invention* (New York: Harcourt Brace World, 1970); Sidney Kaplan, "Jan Matzeliger and the Making of the Shoe," *Journal of Negro History*, ed. William M. Brewer (January, 1955); Frank J. Klingberg, "Carter Goodwin Woodson, Historian, and His Contribution to American Historiography," *Journal of Negro History*, ed. William Brewer (January, 1956); Henry A. Poloski and Roscoe C. Brown, eds., *The Negro Almanac* (New York: Bellwether Publishing Company, 1967); Carter G. Woodson and Charles Wesley, *The Negro in Our History* (Washington, D.C.: The Associated Publishers, 1966); Rackham Holt, *George Washington Carver* (Garden City, New York: Doubleday & Company, 1963); Ben Albert Richardson, *Great American Negroes* (New York: Crowell Publishers, 1945); Roi Ottley, *New World A-Coming* (Boston: Houghton Mifflin Company, 1943); Alain Locke, *The New Negro: An Interpretation* (New York: Albert and Charles Boni, Publishers, 1925); Margaret Just Butcher, *The Negro in American Culture* (New York: Alfred A. Knopf, 1956); Helen Miller Barley, *Forty American Biographies* (New York: Harcourt Brace World, 1964); Russell Adams, *Great Negroes Past and Present* (Chicago: Afro-American Publishing Company, 1964); McKinley Burt, Jr., *Black Inventors of America* (Portland, Oregon: National Book Company).

7. Henry E. Baker, "The Negro in the Field of Invention," *Journal of Negro History* (January, 1917): 17.

8. *The Negro Almanac*, p. 639.

9. *The Negro Almanac,* p. 640.

10. Henry E. Baker, p. 25.

11. Sydney Kaplan, "Jan Matzeliger and the Making of the Shoe," p. 8.

12. Louis Haber, *Black Pioneers of Science and Invention* (New York: Harcourt Brace World, 1970); A. E. Jenkins, *Journal of the Washington Academy of Science,* XXIX (May 15, 1939); G. W. Carver, "Many Food Products Can Be Made from Peanuts and Sweet Potato," *American Food Journal* (August, 1921).

13. Frank J. Klingberg, "Carter Godwin Woodson, Historian, and His Contribution to American Historiography," p. 66; Carter G. Woodson and Charles Wesley, *The Negro in American History* (Washington, D.C.: The Associated Publishers, 1966).

14. E. D. Cronon, *Black Moses* (Madison, Wisconsin: University of Wisconsin Press, 1962); E. U. Essein-Udom, *Black Nationalism* (Chicago: University of Chicago Press, 1962); C. E. Lincoln, *The Black Muslims in America* (Boston: Beacon Press, 1961); W. E. B. Du Bois, "Marcus Garvey," *The Crisis,* XXI (December, 1920 and January, 1921); Amy Jacques-Garvey, ed., *Philosophy and Opinions of Marcus Garvey* (New York, 1923); T. G. Standing, "Nationalism in Negro Leadership," *The American Negro Journal of Sociology,* XL; E. Franklin Frazier, "Garvey: A Mass-Leader," *Nation,* 123 (August 18, 1926) ; Joyce Cary, *The Case for African Freedom* (Austin, Texas: University of Texas Press, 1962); Bennett Lerone, Jr., "The Ghost of Marcus Garvey," *Ebony* (March, 1960).

CHAPTER EIGHT

1. Cf. Alice Rivlin, *Research in the Economics of Higher Education* (Washington, D.C.: The Brookings Institute, 1961), mimeo; Marshall R. Colberg, *Human Capital in Southern Development 1939-1963* (Chapel Hill, North Carolina: University of North Carolina Press, 1965); Andrew G. Frank, *Human Capital and Economic Growth* (New York: Random

House, 1960); Ted Kalem, "Matching Education to Jobs in Developing Nations," *Science,* 160 (June 7, 1968) : 1067-72; George C. Keller, "Biggest Gamble in History: Our Investment in Man," *Reader's Digest,* 93 (December, 1968): 75-79; Hugh McHair, "Education and the Wealth of Nations," *Monthly Labour Review,* 90 (March, 1967): 21-24.

2. Alexander Crummell, "Civilization: The Prime Need of the Race," *American Negro Academy, Occasional Papers,* no. 3 (1897): 3-7.

3. Francis J. Grenike, "Colored Men as Professors in Colored Institutions," *A. M. E. Church Review,* IV (July, 1885) : 142-49.

4. Arthur A. Schomburg, "Racial Integrity: A Plea for the Establishment of a Chair of History in Our Schools and Colleges," *Negro Society for Historical Research, Occasional Papers,* no. 3 (1913): 5-18.

5. Schomburg, pp. 18-19.

6. Cf. Rukudzo Marapa, "Race Pride and Black Political Thought," *Negro Digest* (May, 1969): 6-7.

7. W. E. B. Du Bois, "The Conservation of Races," *American Negro Academy, Occasional Papers,* no. 2 (1897).

8. *Ibid.*

9. To understand W. E. B. Du Bois' educational philosophy it is useful to know his background and views on related subjects. For this reason the following works by Du Bois are recommended: *Darkwater* (New York: Harcourt, Brace and Home, 1920) ; *The Quest of the Silver Fleece* (Chicago: A. C. McClurg, 1911); *The Negro* (New York: Henry Holt and Company, Home University Library of Modern Knowledge, XCI, 1915); *The Gift of Black Folk: Negroes in the Making of America* (Boston: Stratford Company, 1924); "A Negro Schoolmaster in the South," *Atlantic Monthly* (January, 1899); "The Results of the Tuskegee Conferences," *Harper's Weekly* (June 22, 1901); "Of the Training of Black Men," *Atlantic Monthly* (September, 1902); "Possibilities of the Negro: The Advance Guard of the Race," *Booklover's Magazine* (July, 1903); "The Talented Tenth," *The Negro Problem,* ed. Booker T. Washington et al. (New York:

James Pott Company, 1903); "The Training of Negroes for Social Power," *Outlook* (October 17, 1903); "Education and Work," *Howard University Bulletin* (January, 1931); "Social Planning for the Negro: Past and Present," *Journal of Negro Education* (January, 1936); "A Program for Negro Land Grant Colleges" (*Proceedings of the Nineteenth Annual Conference, Presidents of Negro Land Grant Colleges* (Chicago: November, 1941).

10. On Frederick Douglass and his views *see* Philip S. Foner, ed., *Frederick Douglass: Selections from His Writings* (New York: International Publishers Company, 1945), p. 76 f. *Also see* the following works by Frederick Douglass: "To Our Oppressed Countrymen," editorial in the *North Star* (December 3, 1847); "The Future of the Negro," *A. M. E. Review,* VI (October, 1889): 232-33; Benjamin Quarles, *Frederick Douglass* (Washington, D.C.: 1948), p. 334 f.

11. Booker T. Washington, *My Larger Education* (Miami, Florida: Mnemosyne Publishing, 1969) and *The Future of the American Negro* (Boston: Small, Maynard and Company, 1899); George Washington, *Letters and Addresses of George Washington,* ed. Jones Viles (New York: The Unit Book Publishing Company, 1908); J. H. Franklin, *From Slavery to Freedom* (New York: Vintage Book, 1969); H. Hawkins, *Booker T. Washington and His Critics* (New York: D. C. Heath, 1968); E. Thornbrough, *Booker T. Washington* (Englewood Cliffs, New Jersey: Prentice-Hall, 1969).

12. Foner, pp. 90-91.

13. Dwight W. Holmes, *The Evolution of the Negro College* (1934; reprint ed., New York: Arno Press, 1969), pp. 45-46; U.S. Bureau of Education, *Negro Education,* Bulletin 38, vol. 1, pp. 252-53; U.S. Bureau of Education, *Survey of Negro Colleges and Universities,* Bulletin 7 (1928); Horse M. Bone, *The Education of the Negro in the American Social Order* (Englewood Cliffs, New Jersey: Prentice-Hall, 1934), p. 29; Charles S. Johnson, *The Negro College Graduate* (Chapel Hill, North Carolina: University of North Carolina Press, 1938), pp. 92-94; Mary Armstrong, *Hampton and Its Students* (New York: G. P. Putnam's Sons, 1874);

Brown and Poloski, *The Negro Almanac* (New York: Bell-wether Publishing Company, 1967); Kenneth B. Clark, "Higher Education for Negroes: Challenges and Prospects," *Journal of Negro Education,* XXXVI (1967); Virgil A. Clift et al., eds., *Negro Education in America* (New York: Harper & Row, Publishers, 1962); Carter V. Good, *A Guide to Colleges and Universities* (Washington, D.C.: American Council on Education, 1945); Charles S. Johnson, *The Negro College Graduate* (College Park, Maryland: McGrath Publishing Company, 1968); Florence Read, *The Story of Spelman College* (Princeton, New Jersey: Princeton University Press, 1961); Otis Singletary, *American Universities and Colleges* (Washington, D.C.: American Council on Education, 1968) and *Directory of Predominantly Negro Colleges in the United States of America* (Washington, D.C.: Plans for Progress, 1969); American Council on Education, *Intergroup Relations in Teaching Materials* (Menasha, Wisconsin: George Banta Publishing Company, 1949); Francis J. Brown, ed., "Discriminations in College Admissions," *American Council on Education Studies,* ser. I, col. XIX, no. 41 (April, 1950); Nicholas Murray Butler, ed., *Education in the United States,* 2 vols. (1900; reprint ed., New York: Academic Press, Johnson Reprint, 1969); W. E. B. Du Bois, *Black Reconstruction in America* (Cleveland: The World Publishing Company, 1962); Eli Ginzberg, *Manpower Agenda for America* (New York: McGraw-Hill, 1968); Henry J. Perkinson, *The Imperfect Panacea: American Faith in Education 1865-1965* (New York: Random House, 1968); Arnold Rose, *The Negro in America,* the condensed version of Gunnar Myrdal's *An American Dilemma* (New York: Harper & Row, Publishers, 1948); Sargent Shriver and Harold Howe, *Education: An Answer to Poverty* (Washington, D.C.: U.S. Office of Education and the Office of Economic Opportunity, n.d.); Hilda Taba, Elizabeth Brady, and John Robinson, *Intergroup Education in Public Schools* (Washington, D.C.: American Council on Education, 1952); Rena L. Vassar, ed., *Social History of American Education,* vols. I and II (Chicago: Rand McNally and Company, 1965).